Andrew M

Augustine Birrell

Alpha Editions

This edition published in 2024

ISBN : 9789366380186

Design and Setting By
Alpha Editions
www.alphaedis.com
Email - info@alphaedis.com

As per information held with us this book is in Public Domain.
This book is a reproduction of an important historical work. Alpha Editions uses the best technology to reproduce historical work in the same manner it was first published to preserve its original nature. Any marks or number seen are left intentionally to preserve its true form.

Contents

PREFACE .... - 1 -
CHAPTER I .... - 2 -
CHAPTER II .... - 14 -
CHAPTER III .... - 36 -
CHAPTER IV .... - 56 -
CHAPTER V .... - 108 -
CHAPTER VI .... - 128 -
CHAPTER VII .... - 151 -
CHAPTER VIII .... - 162 -

PREFACE

I desire to express my indebtedness to the following editions of Marvell's Works:—

(1) *The Works of Andrew Marvell, Esq., Poetical, Controversial, and Political:* containing many Original Letters, Poems, and Tracts never before printed, with a New Life. By Captain Edward Thompson. In three volumes. London, 1776.

(2) *The Complete Works in Verse and Prose of Andrew Marvell, M.P.* Edited with Memorial-Introduction and Notes by the Rev. Alexander B. Grosart. In four volumes. 1872.

(*In the Fuller Worthies Library.*)

(3) *Poems and Satires of Andrew Marvell, sometime Member of Parliament for Hull.* Edited by G. A. Aitken. Two volumes. Lawrence and Bullen, 1892.

Reprinted Routledge, 1905.

Mr. C. H. Firth's Life of Marvell in the thirty-sixth volume of *The Dictionary of National Biography* has, I am sure, preserved me from some, and possibly from many, blunders.

A. B.

3 NEW SQUARE, LINCOLN'S INN,
June 3, 1905.

CHAPTER I

EARLY DAYS AT SCHOOL AND COLLEGE

THE name of Andrew Marvell ever sounds sweet, and always has, to use words of Charles Lamb's, a fine relish to the ear. As the author of poetry of exquisite quality, where for the last time may be heard the priceless note of the Elizabethan lyricist, whilst at the same moment utterance is being given to thoughts and feelings which reach far forward to Wordsworth and Shelley, Marvell can never be forgotten in his native England.

Lines of Marvell's poetry have secured the final honours, and incurred the peril, of becoming "familiar quotations" ready for use on a great variety of occasion. We may, perhaps, have been bidden once or twice too often to remember how the Royal actor

"Nothing common did, or mean,
Upon that memorable scene,"

or have been assured to our surprise by some self-satisfied worldling how he always hears at his back,

"Time's wingèd chariot hurrying near."

A true poet can, however, never be defiled by the rough usage of the populace.

As a politician Marvell lives in the old-fashioned vivacious history-books (which if they die out, as they show some signs of doing, will carry with them half the historic sense of the nation) as the hero of an anecdote of an unsuccessful attempt made upon his political virtue by a minister of the Crown, as a rare type of an inflexible patriot, and as the last member of the House of Commons who was content to take wages from, instead of contributing to the support of, his constituents. As the intimate friend and colleague of Milton, Marvell shares some of the indescribable majesty of that throne. A poet, a scholar, a traveller, a diplomat, a famous wit, an active member of Parliament from the Restoration to his death in 1678, the life of Andrew Marvell might *a priori* be supposed to be one easy to write, at all events after the fashion in which men's lives get written. But it is nothing of the kind, as many can testify. A more elusive, non-recorded character is hardly to be found. We know all about him, but very little of him. His parentage, his places of education, many of his friends and acquaintances, are all known. He wrote nearly four hundred letters to his Hull constituents, carefully preserved by the Corporation, in which he narrates with much particularity the course of public business at Westminster. Notwithstanding these materials, the man Andrew Marvell remains undiscovered. He rarely comes to the surface. Though both an author and a member of Parliament, not a trace of personal vanity is noticeable, and vanity is a quality of great assistance to the biographer. That Marvell was a strong, shrewd, capable man of affairs, with enormous powers of self-repression, his Hull correspondence clearly proves, but what more he was it is hard to say. He rarely spoke during his eighteen years in the House of Commons. It is impossible to doubt that such a man in such a place was, in Mr. Disraeli's phrase, a "personage." Yet when we look for recognition of what we feel sure was the fact, we fail to find it. Bishop Burnet, in his delightful history, supplies us with sketches of the leading Parliamentarians of Marvell's day, yet to Marvell himself he refers but once, and then not by name but as "the liveliest droll of the age," words which mean much but tell little. In Clarendon's *Autobiography*, another book which lets the reader into the very clash and crowd of life, there is no mention of one of the author's most bitter and cruel enemies. With Prince Rupert, Marvell was credited by his contemporaries with a great intimacy; he was a friend of Harrington's; it may be he was a member of the once famous "Rota" Club; it is impossible to resist the conviction that wherever he went he made a great impression, that he was a central figure in the lobbies of the House of Commons and a man of much account; yet no record survives either to convince posterity of his social charm or even to convey any exact notion of his personal character.

A somewhat solitary man he would appear to have been, though fond of occasional jollity. He lived alone in lodgings, and was much immersed in business, about a good deal of which we know nothing except that it took him abroad. His death was sudden, and when three years afterwards the first edition of his poems made its appearance, it was prefaced by a certificate signed "Mary Marvell," to the effect that everything in the book was printed "according to the copies of my late dear husband." Until after Marvell's death we never hear of Mrs. Marvell, and with this signed certificate she disappears. In a series of Lives of Poets' Wives it would be hard to make much of Mrs. Andrew Marvell. For different but still cogent reasons it is hard to write a life of her famous husband.

Andrew Marvell was born at Winestead in Holdernesse, on Easter Eve, the 31st of March 1621, in the Rectory House, the elder Marvell, also Andrew, being then the parson of the parish. No fitter birthplace for a garden-poet can be imagined. Roses still riot in Winestead; the fruit-tree roots are as mossy as in the seventeenth century. At the right season you may still

"Through the hazels thick espy
The hatching throstle's shining eye."

Birds, fruits and flowers, woods, gardens, meads, and rivers still make the poet's birthplace lovely.

"Loveliness, magic, and grace,
They are here—they are set in the world!
They abide! and the finest of souls
Has not been thrilled by them all,
Nor the dullest been dead to them quite.
The poet who sings them may die,
But they are immortal and live,
For they are the life of the world."

Holdernesse was not the original home of the Marvells, who would seem to have been mostly Cambridgeshire folk, though the name crops up in other counties. Whether Cambridge "men" of a studious turn still take long walks I do not know, but "some vast amount of years ago" it was considered a pleasant excursion, either on foot or on a hired steed, from Cambridge to Meldreth, where the Elizabethan manor-house, long known as "the Marvells'," agreeably embodied the tradition that here it was that the poet's father was born in 1586. The Church Registers have disappeared. Proof is impossible. That there were Marvells in the neighbourhood is certain. The famous Cambridgeantiquary, William Cole, perhaps the greatest of all our collectors, has included among his copies of early wills those of several Marvells and Mervells of Meldreth and Shepreth, belonging to pre-Reformation times, as their pious gifts to the "High Altar" and to "Our Lady's Light" pleasingly testify. But our Andrew was a determined Protestant.

The poet's father is an interesting figure in our Church history. Educated at Emmanuel College, from whence he proceeded a Master of Arts in 1608, he took Orders; and after serving as curate at Flamborough, was inducted to the living of Winestead in 1614, where he remained till 1624, in which year he went to Hull as master of the Grammar School and lecturer, that is preacher, of Trinity Church. The elder Marvell belonged, from the beginning to the end of his useful and even heroic life, to the Reformed Church of England, or, as his son puts it, "a conformist to the Rites and Ceremonies of the Church of England, though I confess none of the most over-running and eager in them." The younger Marvell, with one boyish interval, belonged all through his life to the paternal school of religious thought.

Fuller's account of the elder Marvell is too good to be passed over:—

"He afterwards became Minister at Hull, where for his lifetime he was well beloved. Most facetious in discourse, yet grave in his carriage, a most excellent preacher who, like a good husband, never broached what he had new brewed, but preached what he had pre-studied some competent time before. Insomuch that he was wont to say that he would cross the common proverb which called Saturday the working-day and Monday the holyday of preachers. It happened that Anno Dom. 1640, Jan. 23, crossing Humber in a Barrow boat, the same was sandwarpt, and he was drowned therein (with Mrs. Skinner, daughter to Sir Edward Coke, a very religious gentlewoman) by the carelessness, not to say drunkenness of the boatmen, to the great grief of all good men. His excellent comment upon St. Peter is daily desired and expected, if the envy and covetousness of private persons *for their own use* deprive not the public of the benefit thereof."[1]

This good man, to whom perhaps, remembering the date of his death, the words may apply, *Tu vero felix non vitæ tantum claritate sed etiam opportunitate mortis*, was married at Cherry Burton, on the 22nd of October 1612, to Anne Pease, a member of a family destined to become widely known throughout the north of England. Of this marriage there were five children, all born at Winestead, viz. three daughters, Anne, Mary, and Elizabeth, and two sons, Andrew and John, the latter of whom died a year after his birth, and was buried at Winestead on the 20th September 1624.

The three daughters married respectively James Blaydes of Sutton, Yorkshire, on the 29th of December 1633; Edmund Popple, afterwards Sheriff of Hull, on the 18th of August 1636; and Robert More. Anne's eldest son, Joseph Blaydes, was Mayor of Hull in 1702, having married the daughter of a preceding Mayor in 1698. The descendants of this branch still flourish. The Popples also had children, one of whom, William Popple, was a correspondent of his uncle the poet's, and a merchant of repute, who became in 1696 Secretary to the Board of Trade, and the friend of the most famous man who ever sat at the table of that Board, John Locke. A son of this William Popple led a very comfortable eighteenth-century life, which is in strong contrast with that of his grand-uncle, for, having entered the Cofferers' Office about 1730, he was made seven years later Solicitor and Clerk of the Reports to the Commissioners of Trade and Plantations, and in 1745 became in succession to a relative, one Alured Popple, Governor of the Bermudas, a post he retained until his death, which occurred not

"Where the remote Bermudas ride
In the ocean's bosom unespied,"

but at his house in Hampstead. So well placed and idle a gentleman was almost bound to be a bad poet and worse dramatist, and this William Popple was both.

Marvell's third sister, Elizabeth, does not seem to have had issue, a certain Thomas More, or Moore, a Fellow of Magdalen College, Cambridge, whose name occurs in family records, being her stepson.

In the latter part of 1624 the elder Marvell resigned the living of Winestead, and took up the duties of schoolmaster and lecturer, or preacher, at Hull. Important duties they were, for the old Grammar School of Hull dates back to 1486, and may boast of a long career of usefulness, never having fallen into that condition of decay and disrepute from which so many similar endowments have been of late years rescued by the beneficent and, of course, abused action of the Charity Commissioners. Andrew Marvell the elder succeeded to and was succeeded by eminent headmasters. Trinity Church, where the poet's father preached on Sundays to crowded and interested congregations, was then what it still is, though restored by Scott, one of the great churches in the north of England.

The Rev. Andrew Marvell made his mark upon Hull. Mr. Grosart, who lacked nothing but the curb upon a too exuberant vocabulary, a little less enthusiasm and a great deal more discretion, to be a model editor, tells us in his invaluable edition of *The Complete Works in Verse and Prose of Andrew Marvell, M.P.*,[1] that he had read a number of the elder Marvell's manuscripts, consisting of sermons and miscellaneous papers, from which Mr. Grosart proceeds:—

"I gather three things.

"(1) That he was a man of a very brave, fearlessly outspoken character. Some of his practical applications in his sermons before the Magistrates are daring in their directness of reproof, and melting in their wistfulness of entreaty.

"(2) That he was a well-read man. His Sermons are as full of classical and patristic allusions and pat sayings from the most occult literatures as even Bishop Andrewes.

"(3) That he was a man of tireless activity. Besides the two offices named, he became head of one of the Great Hospitals of the Town (Charter House), and in an address to the Governors placed before them a prescient and statesmanlike plan for the better management of its revenues, and for the foundation of a Free Public Library to be accessible to all."

When at a later day, and in the midst of a fierce controversy, Andrew Marvell wrote of the clergy as "the reserve of our Christianity," he doubtless had such men as his father in his mind and memory.

It was at the old Grammar School of Hull, and with his father as his *Orbilius*, that Marvell was initiated into the mysteries of the Latin grammar, and was, as he tells us, put to his

"Montibus, inquit, erunt; et erant submontibus illis;
Risit Atlantiades; et me mihi, perfide, prodis?
Me mihi prodis? ait.

"For as I remember this scanning was a liberal art that we learn'd at Grammar School, and to scan verses as he does the Author's prose before we did or were obliged to understand them."[2]

Irrational methods have often amazingly good results, and the Hull Grammar School provided its head-master's only son with the rudiments of learning, thus enabling him to become in after years what John Milton himself, the author of that terrible *Treatise on Education* addressed to Mr. Hartlibb, affirmed Andrew Marvell to be in a written testimonial, "a scholar, and well-read in the Latin and Greek authors."

Attached to the Grammar School there was "a great garden," renowned for its wall-fruit and flowers; so by leaving Winestead behind, our "garden-poet," that was to be, was not deprived of inspiration.

Apart from these meagre facts, we know nothing of Marvell's boyhood at Hull. His clerical foe, Dr. Parker, afterwards Bishop of Oxford, writes contemptuously of "an hunger-starved whelp of a country vicar," and in another passage, which undoubtedly refers to Marvell, he speaks of "an unhappy education among Boatswains and Cabin-boys," whose unsavoury phrases, he goes on to suggest, Marvell picked up in his childhood. But truth need not be looked for in controversial pages. The best argument for a married clergy is to be found, for Englishmen at all events, in the sixty-seven volumes of the *Dictionary of National Biography*, where are recorded the services rendered to religion, philosophy, poetry, justice, and the empire by the "whelps" of many a country vicar. Parsons' wives may sometimes be trying and hard to explain, but an England without the sons of her clergy would be shorn of half her glory.

Marvell's boyhood seems to have been surrounded with the things that most make for a child's happiness. A sensible, affectionate, humorous, religious father, occupying a position of authority, and greatly respected, a mother and three elder sisters to make much of his bright wit and early adventures, a comfortable yet simple home, and an atmosphere of piety, learning, and good fellowship. What more is wanted, or can be desired? The "Boatswains" and "Cabin-boys" of Bishop Parker's fancy were in the neighbourhood, no doubt, and as stray companions for a half-holiday must have had their attractions; but it is unnecessary to attribute Andrew Marvell's style in controversy to his early acquaintance with a sea-faring population, for he is far more likely to have picked it up from his great friend and colleague, the author of *Paradise Lost*.

Marvell's school education over, he went up to Cambridge, not to his father's old college, but to the more splendid foundation of Trinity. About the date of his matriculation there is a doubt. In Wood's *Athenæ Oxonienses* there is a note to the effect that Marvell was admitted "in matriculam Acad. Cant. Coll. Trin." on the 14th of December 1633, when the boy was but twelve years old. Dr. Lort, a famous master of Trinity in his day, writing in November 1765 to Captain Edward Thompson, of whom more later on, told the captain that until 1635 there was no register of admissions of ordinary students, or pensioners, as they are called, but only a register of Fellows and Foundation Scholars, and in this last-named register Marvell's name appears as a Scholar sworn and admitted on the 13th of April 1638. As, however, Marvell took his B.A. degree in 1639, he must have been in residence long before April 1638. Probably Marvell went to Trinity about 1635, just before the register of pensioners was begun, as a pensioner, becoming a Scholar in 1638, and taking his degree in 1639.

Cambridge undergraduates do not usually keep diaries, nor after they have become Masters of Art are they much in the habit of giving details as to their academic career. Marvell is no exception to this provoking rule. He nowhere tells us what his University taught him or how. The logic of the schools he had no choice but to learn. Molineus, Peter Ramus, Seton, Keckerman were text-books of reputation, from one or another of which every Cambridge man had to master his *simpliciters*, his *quids*, his *secundum quids*, his *quales*, and his *quantums*. Aristotle's Physics, Ethics, and Politics were "tutor's books," and those young men who loved to hear themselves talk were left free to discuss, much to Hobbes's disgust, "the freedom of the will, incorporeal substance, everlasting nows, ubiquities, hypostases, which the people understand not nor will ever care for."

In the life of Matthew Robinson,[1] who went up to Cambridge a little later than Marvell (June 1645), and was probably a harder reader, we are told that "the strength of his studies lay in the metaphysics and in those subtle authors for many years which rendered him an irrefragable disputant *de quolibet ente*, and whilst he was but senior freshman he was found in the bachelor schools, disputing ably with the best of the senior sophisters." Robinson despised the old-fashioned Ethics and Physics, but with the new Cartesian or Experimental Philosophy he was *inter primos*. History, particularly the Roman, was in great favour at both Universities at this time, and young men were taught, so old Hobbes again grumbles, to despise monarchy "from Cicero, Seneca, Cato and other politicians of Rome, and Aristotle of Athens, who seldom spake of kings but as of wolves and other ravenous beasts."[1] The Muses were never neglected at Cambridge, as the University exercises survive to prove, whilst modern languages, Spanish and Italian for example, were greedily acquired by such an eager spirit as Richard Crashaw, the poet, who came into residence at Pembroke in 1631. There were problems to be "kept" in the college chapel, lectures to be attended, both public and private, declamations to be delivered, and even in the vacations the scholars were not exempt from "exercises" either in hall or in their tutors' rooms. Earnest students read their Greek Testaments, and even their Hebrew Bibles, and filled their note-books, working more hours a day than was good for their health, whilst the idle ones wasted their time as best they could in an unhealthy, over-crowded town, in an age which knew nothing of boating, billiards, or cricket. A tennis-court there was in Marvell's time, for in Dr. Worthington's *Diary*, under date 3rd of April 1637, it stands recorded that on that day and in that place that learned man received "a dangerous blow on the Eye."[2]

The only incident we know of Marvell's undergraduate days is remarkable enough, for, boy though he was, he seems, like the Gibbon of a later day, to have suddenly become a Roman Catholic. This occurrence may serve to remind us how, during Marvell's time at Trinity, the University of Cambridge (ever the precursor in thought-movements) had a Catholic revival of her own, akin to that one which two hundred years afterwards happened at Oxford, and has left so much agreeable literature behind it. Fuller in his history of the University of Cambridge tells us a little about this highly interesting and important movement:—

"Now began the University (1633-4) to be much beautified in buildings, every college either casting its skin with the snake, or renewing its bill with the eagle, having their courts or at least their fronts and Gatehouses repaired and adorned. But the greatest alteration was in their Chapels, most of them being graced with the accession of organs. And seeing musick is one of the liberal arts, how could it be quarrelled at in an University if they sang with understanding both of the matter and manner thereof. Yet some took great distaste thereat as attendancie to superstition."[1]

The chapel at Peterhouse, we read elsewhere, which was built in 1632, and consecrated by Bishop White of Ely, had a beautiful ceiling and a noble east window. "A grave divine," Fuller tells us, "preaching before the University at St. Mary's, had this smart passage in his Sermon—that as at the Olympian Games he was counted the Conqueror who could drive his chariot wheels nearest the mark yet so as not to hinder his running or to stick thereon, so he who in his Sermons could preach *near Popery* and yet *no Popery, there was your man*. And indeed it now began to be the general complaint of most moderate men that many in the University, both in the schools and pulpits, approached the opinions of the Church of Rome nearer than ever before."

Archbishop Laud, unlike the bishops of Dr. Newman's day, favoured the Catholic revival, and when Mr. Bernard, the lecturer of St. Sepulchre's,

London, preached a "No Popery" sermon at St. Mary's, Cambridge, he was dragged into the High Commission Court, and, as the hateful practice then was, a practice dear to the soul of Laud, was bidden to subscribe a formal recantation. This Mr. Bernard refused to do, though professing his sincere sorrow and penitence for any oversights and hasty expressions in his sermon. Thereupon he was sent back to prison, where he died. "If," adds Fuller, "he was miserably abused in prison by the keepers (as some have reported) to the shortening of his life, He that maketh inquisition for blood either hath or will be a revenger thereof."[1]

By the side of this grim story the much-written-about incidents of the Oxford Movement seem trivial enough.

Not a few Cambridge scholars of this period, Richard Crashaw among the number, found permanent refuge in Rome.

The story of Marvell's conversion is emphatic but vague in its details. The "Jesuits," who were well represented in Cambridge at the time, are said to have persuaded him to leave Cambridge secretly, and to take refuge in one of their houses in London. Thither the elder Marvell followed in pursuit, and after search came across his son in a bookseller's shop, where he succeeded both in convincing the boy of his errors and in persuading him to return to Trinity. An odd story, and not, as it stands, very credible; but Mr. Grosart discovered among the Marvell papers at Hull a fragment of a letter without signature, address, or date, which throws some sort of light on the incident. This letter was evidently, as Mr. Grosart surmises, sent to the elder Marvell by some similarly afflicted parent. In its fragmentary state the letter reads as follows:—

"Worthy S^r,—Mr Breerecliffe being wth me to-day, I related vnto him a fearfull passage lately at Cambridg touching a sonne of mine, Bachelor of Arts in Katherine Hall, wch was this. He was lately inuited to a supper in towne by a gentlewoman, where was one Mr Nichols a felow of Peterhouse, and another or two masters of arts, I know not directly whether felowes or not: my sonne hauing noe p'ferment, but liuing meerely of my penny, they pressed him much to come to liue at their house, and for chamber and extraordinary bookes they promised farre: and then earnestly moued him to goe to Somerset house, where they could doe much for p'ferring him to some eminent place, and in conclusion to popish arguments to seduce him soe rotten and vnsauory as being ouerheard it was brought in question before the heads of the Uniuersity: *Dr. Cosens*, being *Vice Chancelor* noe punishment is inioined him: but on Ash-wednesday next a recantation in regent house of some popish tenets Nicols let fall: I p'ceive by Mr Breercliffe some such prank vsed towards y^r sonne: I desire to know what y^u did therin: thinking I cannot doe god better seruice then bring it vppon the stage either in

Parliament if it hold: or informing some Lords of the Counsail to whom I stand much oblieged if a bill in Starchamber be meete To terrify others by making these some publique spectacle: for if such fearfull practises may goe vnpunished I take care whether I may send a child ... the lord."[1]

The reference to Dr. Cosens, or Cosin, being Vice-Chancellor gives a clue to the date, for Cosin was chosen Vice-Chancellor on the 4th of November 1639.[2]

Though we can know nothing of the elder Marvell's methods of re-conversion, they were more successful than the elder Gibbon's, who, as we know, packed the future historian off to Lausanne and a Swiss pastor's house. What Gibbon became on leaving off his Romanism we can guess for ourselves, whereas Marvell, once out of the hands of these very shadowy "Jesuits," remained the staunchest of Christian Protestants to the end of his days.

This strange incident, and two college exercises or poems, one in Greek, the other in Latin, both having reference to an addition to the Royal Family, and appearing in the *Musa Cantabrigiensis* for 1637, are all the materials that exist for weaving the story of Marvell, the Cambridge undergraduate. The Latin verses, which are Horatian in style, contain one pretty stanza, composed apparently before the sex of the new-born infant was known at Cambridge.

"Sive felici Carolum figurâ
Parvulus princeps imitetur almae
Sive Mariae decoret puellamDulcis imago."

After taking his Bachelor's degree in 1639, Marvell, being still a Scholar of the college, must have gone away, for the Conclusion Book of Trinity, under date September 24, 1641, records as follows:—

"It is agreed by ye Master and 8 seniors y^t Mr Carter and Dr Wakefields, Dr Marvell, Dr Waterhouse, and Dr Maye in regard y^t some of them are reported to be married and y^t others look not after y^eir days nor Acts shall receave no more benefitt of ye Coll and shall be out of y^ier places unless y^ei shew just cause to ye Coll for ye contrary in 3 months."

Dr. Lort, in his amiable letter of 1765, already mentioned, points out that this entry contains no reflection on Marvell's morals, but shows that he was given "notice to quit" for non-residence, "then much more strictly enjoined than it is now." The days referred to in the entry were, so the master obligingly explains, "the certain number allowed by statute to absentees," whilst the "acts mean the Exercises also enjoyed by the statutes." Dr. Lort adds, "It does not appear, by any subsequent entry, whether Marvell did or did not comply with this order." We may now safely assume he did not. Marvell's Cambridge days were over.

The vacations, no inconsiderable part of the year, were probably spent by Marvell under his father's roof at Hull, where his two elder sisters were married and settled. It is not to be wondered at that Andrew Marvell should, for so many years, have represented Hull in the House of Commons, for both he and his family were well known in the town. The elder Marvell added to his reputation as a teacher and preacher the character of a devoted servant of his flock in the hour of danger. The plague twice visited Hull during the time of the elder Marvell, first in 1635 and again in 1638. In those days men might well pray to be delivered from "plague, pestilence, and famine." Hull suffered terribly on both occasions. We have seen, in comparatively recent times, the effect of the cholera upon large towns, and the plague was worse than the cholera many times over. The Hull preacher, despite the stigma of *facetiousness*, which still clings to him, stuck to his post, visiting the sick, burying the dead, and even, which seems a little superfluous, preaching and afterwards printing "by request" their funeral sermons. A brave man, indeed, and one reserved for a tragic end.

In April 1638 the poet's mother died. In the following November the elder Marvell married a widow lady, but his own end was close upon him. The earliest consecutive account of this strange event is in Gent's *History of Hull* (1735):—"This year, 1640, the Rev. Mr. Andrew Marvell, Lecturer of Hull, sailing over the Humber in company with Madame Skinner of Thornton College and a young beautiful couple who were going to be wedded; a speedy Fate prevented the designed happy union thro' a violent storm which overset the boat and put a period to all their lives, nor were there any remains of them or the vessel ever after found, tho' earnestly sought for on distant shores."

Thus died by drowning a brave man, a good Christian, and an excellent clergyman of the Reformed Church of England. The plain narrative just quoted has been embroidered by many long-subsequent writers in the interests of those who love presentiments and ghostly intimations of impending events, and in one of these versions it is recorded, that though the morning was clear, the breeze fair, and the company gay, yet when stepping into the boat "the reverend man exclaimed, 'Ho for Heaven,' and threw his staff ashore and left it to Providence to fulfil its awful warning."

So melancholy an occurrence naturally excited great attention, and long lingered in local memories. Everybody in Hull knew who was their member's father.

There is an obstinate tradition quite unverifiable that Mrs. Skinner, the mother of the beautiful young lady who was drowned with the elder Marvell, adopted the young Marvell as a son, sending to Cambridge for him after his father's death, and providing him with the means of travel, and that afterwards she bequeathed him her estate. Whether there is any truth in this story cannot now be ascertained. The Skinners were a well-known Hull family, one of them, a brother of that Cyriac Skinner who was urged by Milton in immortal verse to enjoy himself whilst the mood was on him, having been Mayor of Hull. The lady, doubtless, had money, and Andrew Marvell was in need of money, and appears to have been supplied with it. It is quite possible the tradition is true.

[6:1] Fuller's *Worthies* (1662), p. 159.

[8:1] "The Fuller Worthies Library," 4 vols., 1872. Hereafter referred to as *Grosart*.

[8:2] *Mr. Smirke or the Divine in Mode.*—Grosart, iv. 15.

[11:1] *Autobiography of Matthew Robinson.* Edited by J. E. B. Mayor, Cambridge, 1856.

[12:1] *Behemoth*, Hobbes' Works (Molesworth), vol. vi., see pp. 168, 218, 233-6.

[12:2] Worthington's *Diary*, vol. i. p. 5 (Chetham Society).

[13:1] Fuller, *History of Cambridge University* (1655), p. 167.

[14:1] Fuller, p. 166.

[15:1] Grosart, I., xxviii.

[15:2] See Worthington's *Diary*, vol. i. p. 7.

CHAPTER II

"THE HAPPY GARDEN-STATE"

THE seventeenth century was the century of travel for educated Englishmen—of long, leisurely travel. Milton's famous Italian tour lasted fifteen months. John Evelyn's *Wander-Jahre* occupied four years. Andrew Marvell lived abroad in France, Spain, Holland, and Italy from 1642 to 1646, and we have Milton's word for it that when the traveller returned he was well acquainted with the French, Dutch, Spanish, and Italian languages. Andrew Marvell was a highly cultivated man, living in a highly cultivated age, in daily converse with scholars, poets, philosophers, and men of very considerable scientific attainments. In reading Clarendon and Burnet, and whilst turning over Aubrey's delightful gossip, it is impossible not to be struck with the width and variety of the learning as well as with the wit of the period. Intellectually it was a great age.

No record remains of Marvell's travels during these years. Up and down his writings the careful reader will come across pleasant references to foreign manners and customs, betokening the keen humorous observer, and the possession of that wide-eyed faculty that takes a pleasure, half contemplative, half the result of animal spirits, in watching the way of the world wherever you may chance to be. Of another and an earlier traveller, Sir Henry Wotton, we read in "Walton's *Life*."

"And whereas he was noted in his youth to have a sharp wit and apt to jest, *that* by time, travel, and conversation was so polished and made useful, that his company seemed to be one of the delights of mankind."

In all Marvell's work, as poet, as Parliamentarian, as controversialist, we shall see the travelled man. Certainly no one ever more fully grasped the sense of the famous sentence given by Wotton to Milton, when the latter was starting on his travels: "*I pensieri stretti ed il viso sciolto.*"

Marvell was in Rome about 1645. I can give no other date during the whole four years. This, our only date, rests upon an assumption. In Marvell's earliest satirical poem he gives an account of a visit he paid in Rome to the unlucky poetaster Flecknoe, who was not in Rome until 1645. If, therefore, the poem records an actual visit, it follows that the author of the poem was in Rome at the same time. It is not very near, but it is as near as we can get.

Richard Flecknoe was an Irish priest of blameless life, with a passion for scribbling and for printing. His exquisite reason for both these superfluous acts is worth quoting:—

"I write chiefly to avoid idleness, and print to avoid the imputation (of idleness), and as others do it to live after they are dead, I do it only not to be thought dead whilst I am alive."[1]

Such frankness should have disarmed ridicule, but somehow or another this amiable man came to be regarded as the type of a dull author, and his name passed into a proverb for stupidity, so much so that when Dryden in 1682 was casting about how best to give pain to Shadwell, he devised the plan of his famous satire, "MacFlecknoe," where in biting verse he describes Flecknoe (who was happily dead) as an aged Prince—

"Who like Augustus young
Was called to empire and had governed long;
In prose and verse was owned, without dispute,
Through all the realms of nonsense absolute."

Dryden goes on to picture the aged Flecknoe,

"pondering which of all his sons was fit
To reign and wage immortal war with Wit,"

and fixing on Shadwell.

"Shadwell alone my perfect image bears,
Mature in dulness from his tender years;
Shadwell alone, of all my sons, is he
Who stands confirmed in full stupidity:
The rest to some faint meaning make pretence,
But Shadwell never deviates into sense."

Thus has it come about that Flecknoe, the Irish priest, whom Marvell visited in his Roman garret in 1645, bears a name ever memorable in literature.

Marvell's own poem, though eclipsed by the splendour of Glorious John's resounding lines, has an interest of its own as being, in its roughly humorous way, a forerunner of the "Dunciad" and "Grub Street" literature, by which in sundry moods 'tis "pleasure to be bound." It describes seeking out the poetaster in his lodging "three staircases high," at the sign of the Pelican, in a room so small that it seemed "a coffin set in the stair's head." No sooner was the rhymer unearthed than straightway he began to recite his poetry in dismal tones, much to his visitor's dismay:—

"But I who now imagin'd myself brought
To my last trial, in a serious thought

Calm'd the disorders of my youthful breast
And to my martyrdom preparèd rest.
Only this frail ambition did remain,
The last distemper of the sober brain,
That there had been some present to assure
The future ages how I did endure."

To stop the cataract of "hideous verse," Marvell invited the scarecrow to dinner, and waits while he dresses. As they turn to leave, for the room is so small that the man who comes in last must be the first to go out, they meet a friend of the poet on the stairs, who makes a third at dinner. After dinner Flecknoe produces ten quires of paper, from which the friend proceeds to read, but so infamously as to excite their author's rage:—

"But all his praises could not now appease
The provok't Author, whom it did displease
To hear his verses by so just a curse
That were ill made, condemned to be read worse:
And how (impossible!) he made yet more
Absurdities in them than were before:
For his untun'd voice did fall or raise
As a deaf man upon the Viol plays,
Making the half-points and the periods run
Confus'der than the atoms in the sun:
Thereat the poet swell'd with anger full,"

and after violent exclamations retires in dudgeon back to his room. The faithful friend is in despair. What is he to do to make peace? "Who would commend his mistress now?" Marvell

"counselled him to go in time
Ere the fierce poet's anger turned to rhyme."

The advice was taken, and Marvell, finding himself at last free from boredom, went off to St. Peter's to return thanks.

This poem is but an unsatisfactory *souvenir de voyage*, but it is all there is.

What Marvell was doing during the stirring years 1646-1650 is not known. Even in the most troubled times men go about their business, and our poet was always a man of affairs. As for his opinions during these years, we can only guess at them from those to which he afterwards gave expression. Marvell was neither a Republican nor a Puritan. Like his father before him, he was a Protestant and a member of the Reformed Church of England. He stood for both King and Parliament. Archbishop Laud he distrusted, and it may well be detested, but good churchmen have often distrusted and even detested their archbishops. Mr. Gladstone had no great regard for Archbishop Tait. Before the Act of Uniformity and the repressive legislation that followed upon its heels had driven English dissent into its final moulds, it was not doctrine but ceremonies that disturbed men's minds; and Marvell belonged to that school of English churchmen, by no means the least distinguished school, which was not disposed to quarrel with their fellow-Christians over white surplices, the ring in matrimony, or the attitude during Holy Communion. He shared the belief of a contemporary that no system is bad enough to destroy a good man, or good enough to save a bad one.

The Civil War was to Marvell what it was to most wise men not devoured by faction—a deplorable event. Twenty years after he wrote in the *Rehearsal Transprosed*:—

"Whether it be a war of religion or of liberty it is not worth the labour to inquire. Whichsoever was at the top, the other was at the bottom; but upon considering all, I think the cause was too good to have been fought for. Men ought to have trusted God—they ought to have trusted the King with that whole matter. The arms of the Church are prayers and tears, the arms of the subject are patience and petitions. The King himself being of so accurate and piercing a judgment would soon have felt it where it stuck. For men may spare their pains when Nature is at work, and the world will not go the faster for our driving. Even as his present Majesty's happy Restoration did itself, so all things else happen in their best and proper time, without any heed of our officiousness."[1]

In the face of this passage and many another of the like spirit, it is puzzling to find such a man, for example, as Thomas Baker, the ejected non-juring Fellow and historian of St. John's College, Cambridge (1656-1740), writing of Marvell as "that bitter republican"; and Dryden, who probably knew Marvell, comparing his controversial pamphlets with those of Martin Marprelate, or at all events speaking of Martin Marprelate as "the Marvell of those times."[2] A somewhat anti-prelatical note runs through Marvell's writings, but it is a familiar enough note in the works of the English laity, and by no means dissevers its possessor from the Anglican Church. But there are some heated expressions in the satires which probably gave rise to the belief that Marvell was a Republican.[3]

During the Commonwealth Marvell was content to be a civil servant. He entertained for the Lord-Protector the same kind of admiration that such a loyalist as Chateaubriand could not help feeling for Napoleon. Even Clarendon's pedantic soul occasionally vibrates as he writes of Oliver, and compares his reputation in foreign courts with that of his own royal master.

When the Restoration came Marvell rejoiced. Two old-established things had been destroyed by Cromwell—Kings and Parliaments, and Marvell was glad to see them both back again in England.

Some verses of Marvell's attributable to this period (1646-1650) show him keeping what may be called Royalist company. With a dozen other friends of Richard Lovelace, the Cavalier poet and the author of two of the most famous stanzas in English verse, Marvell contributed some commendatory lines addressed to his "noble friend, Mr. Richard Lovelace, upon his Poems," which appeared with the poems themselves in that year of fate, 1649. "After the murder of the King," says Anthony Wood, "Lovelace was set at liberty, and having by that time consumed all his estate, grew very melancholy, became very poor in body and purse, was the object of charity, went in ragged clothes (whereas when he was in glory he wore cloth of gold and silver), and mostly lodged in obscure and dirty places, more befitting the worst of beggars and poorest of servants."

Then it was that *Lucasta* made its first appearance. When the fortunes of the gallant poet were at their lowest and never to revive, Marvell seizes the occasion to deplore the degeneracy of the times, a familiar theme with poets:—

"Our civil wars have lost the civic crown,
He highest builds who with most art destroys,
And against others' fame his own employs."

He then glances scornfully at the new Presbyterian censorship of the press:—

"The barbèd censurers begin to look
Like the grim consistory on thy book,
And on each line cast a reforming eye,"

and suggests that *Lucasta* is in danger because in 1642 its author had been imprisoned by order of the House of Commons for presenting a petition from Kent which prayed for the restoration of the Book of Common Prayer. This danger is, however, overcome by the ladies, who rise in arms to defend their favourite poet.

"But when the beauteous Ladies came to know
That their dear Lovelace was endangered so,
Lovelace that thaw'd the most congealèd breast,
He who lov'd best and them defended best,
They all in mutiny, though yet undrest,Sally'd."

One of them challenged Marvell as to whether he had not been of the poet's traducers, but he answered No!

"O No, mistake not, I reply'd, for I
In your defence or in his cause would die.
But he, secure of glory and of time,
Above their envy or my aid doth climb.
Him, bravest men and fairest nymphs approve,
His book in them finds Judgment, with you, Love."

Lovelace did not live to see the Restoration, but died in a mean lodging near Shoe Lane in April 1658, and was buried in St. Bridget's Church. Let us indulge the hope that the friends who occupied so many of the introductory pages of Lovelace's *Lucasta* occasionally enlivened the solitude and relieved the distress of the poet whose praises they had once sung with so much vigour. As Marvell was undoubtedly a friendly man, and one who loved to be alone with his friends, and had never any house of his own to keep up, living for the most part in hired lodgings, it would be unkind to doubt that he at least did not forget Lovelace in his poverty and depression of spirit.

In 1649 thirty-three poets combined to weep over the early grave of the Lord Henry Hastings, the eldest son of the sixth Earl of Huntingdon, who died of the smallpox in the twentieth year of his age. Not even this plentiful discharge of poets' tears should rob the young nobleman of his claim to be regarded as a fine example of the great learning, accomplishments, and high spirits of the age. We can still produce the thirty-three poets, but what young nobleman is there who can boast such erudition as had rewarded the scorned delights and the laborious days of this Lord Hastings? We have at least the satisfaction of knowing that did such a one exist he probably would not die of the smallpox. Among the poets who wept on this occasion were Herrick, Sir John Denham, Andrew Marvell, and John Dryden, then a Westminster schoolboy, whose description of the smallpox is as bad as the disease.

Marvell's verses begin very prettily and soon introduce a characteristic touch:—

"Go, stand betwixt the Morning and the Flowers,
And ere they fall arrest the early showers,
Hastings is dead; and we disconsolate
With early tears must mourn his early fate."

In 1650 Marvell, then in his twenty-ninth year, went to live with Lord Fairfax at Nunappleton House in Yorkshire, as tutor to the only child and daughter of the house, Mary Fairfax, aged twelve years (born 30th July 1638). This proved to be a great event in Marvell's life as a poet, and it happened at an epoch in the distinguished career of the famous Parliamentarian general

"Whose name in arms through Europe rings."

Lord Fairfax, though he had countenanced, if not approved, the trial and deposition of the king, had resolutely held himself aloof from the proceedings which, beginning on Saturday the 20th of January 1649, terminated so dismally on Tuesday the 30th. The strange part played by Lady Fairfax on the first day of the so-called trial (though it was no greater a travesty of justice than many a real trial both before and after) is one of the best-known stories in English history. There are several versions of it. Having provided herself with a seat in a small gallery in Westminster Hall, just above the heads of the judges, when her husband's name was called out as one of the commissioners, the intrepid lady (no Cavalier's dame, be it remembered, but a true blue Presbyterian), a brave soldier's daughter, cried out, "Lord Fairfax is not here; he will never sit among you. You do wrong to name him as a sitting Commissioner." This is Rushworth's version, and he was present. Clarendon, who was not present, being abroad at the time, reports the words as, "He has more wit than to be here."

Later on in the day, when the President Bradshaw interrupted the king and peremptorily bade him to answer the charges exhibited against him "in the name of the Commons of England assembled, and of the people of England," Lady Fairfax again rose to her feet and exclaimed, "It's a lie! Not half the people. Where are they and their consents? Oliver Cromwell is a traitor."

Lieutenant-Colonel Axtell, who during the trial was in command of a regiment in Westminster and charged by his military superior, Lord Fairfax himself, with the duty of maintaining order, hearing this disturbance, went forward and told Lady Fairfax to hold her tongue, sound advice which she appears to have taken. After the Restoration Axtell was put to his trial as a "regicide." His defence, which was, that as a soldier he obeyed his orders, and was no more guilty than his general, Lord Fairfax, was not listened to, and he was sentenced to death, a fate which he met like the brave man he was.

Although Fairfax did not immediately resign his command after the king's death, from that moment he lost heart in the cause. Lady Fairfax, whose loyalty to Charles may have been quickened by her dislike of Oliver, had great influence with him, and it may well be that his conscience pricked him. The rupture came in June 1650, when Charles's son made his appearance in Scotland and his peace with the Presbyterians, subscribing with inward emotions it would be unkind to attempt to describe the Solemn League and

Covenant, and attending services and listening to sermons the length of which, at least, he never forgot. War was plainly imminent between the two countries. The question was, who should begin? Cromwell, who had hurried home from Ireland, Lambert, and Harrison were all keen to strike the first blow. Fairfax felt a scruple, and in those days scruples counted. Was there, he asked, a just cause for an invasion of Scotland? A committee was appointed, consisting of the three warriors above-named with St. John and Whitelock, to confer with the Lord-General and satisfy him of the lawfulness of the undertaking. The six met, and having first prayed—Oliver praying first—they proceeded to a discussion which may be read at length in Whitelock's *Memorials*, vol. iii. p. 207. The substance of their talk was as follows: Fairfax's scruple proved to be that both they and the Scots had joined in the Solemn League and Covenant, and that, therefore, until Scotland assumed the offensive, there was no cause for an invasion. Cromwell's retort, after a preliminary quibble, was practical enough. "War is inevitable. Is it better to have it in the bowels of another's country or in one's own? In one or other it must be." Fairfax's scruple, however, withstood this battery, though it was strongly enforced by Harrison, who, in reply to the Lord-General's question, "What was the warrant for the assumption that Scotland meant to fall upon England?" inquired, if Scotland did not mean to invade England, for whose benefit were levies being made and soldiers enlisted.

Fairfax proved immovable. "Every man," said he, "must stand or fall by his own conscience"; and as he offered to lay down his command, there was nothing for it but to accept the resignation and appoint his successor. This was speedily done, and on the 28th of June 1650 "Oliver Cromwell, Esquire," was appointed Captain-General and Commander-in-chief of all the forces. On 16th July Cromwell crossed the Tweed, and on the 3rd of September the Lord delivered Leslie into his hands at Dunbar.

It was in these circumstances that Lord Fairfax and his energetic lady and only child went back to their Yorkshire home in the midsummer of 1650, taking Marvell with them to instruct the Lady Mary in the tongues.

Nunappleton House is in the Ainstey of York, a pleasant bit of country bounded by the rivers Ouse, Wharfe, and Nidd. The modern traveller, as his train rushes north, whilst shut up in his corridor-carriage with his rug, his pipe, and his novel, passes at no great distance from the house on the way between Selby and York. The old house, as it was in Marvell's time, is thus described by Captain Markham, who had a print to help him, in his delightful *Life of the Great Lord Fairfax*:—

"It was a picturesque brick mansion with stone copings and a high steep roof, and consisted of a centre and two wings at right angles, forming three sides of a square, facing to the north. The great hall or gallery occupied the centre between the two wings. It was fifty yards long, and was adorned with thirty shields in wood, painted with the arms of the family. In the three rooms there were chimney-pieces of delicate marble of various colours, and many fine portraits on the walls. The central part of the house was surrounded by a cupola, and clustering chimneys rose in the two wings. A noble park with splendid oak-trees, and containing 300 head of deer, stretched away to the north, while on the south side were the ruins of the old Nunnery, the flower-garden, and the low meadows called *ings* extending to the banks of the Wharfe. In this flower-garden the General took especial delight. The flowers were planted in masses, tulips, pinks, and roses, each in separate beds, which were cut into the shape of forts with five bastions. General Lambert, whom Fairfax had reared as a soldier, also loved his flowers, and excelled both in cultivating them and in painting them from Nature. Lord Fairfax only went to Denton, the favourite seat of his grandfather, when the floods were out over the *ings* at Nunappleton, and he also occasionally resorted to his house at Bishop Hill in York."[1]

In this garden the muse of Andrew Marvell blossomed like the cherry-tree.

Lord Fairfax, though furious in war, and badly wounded in many a fierce engagement, was, when otherwise occupied, a man of quiet literary tastes, and a good bit of a collector and *virtuoso*. Some of the rare books and manuscripts he had around him at Nunappleton are now in the Bodleian, the treasures of which he had protected in troubled times. He loved to handle medals and coins, and knew the points of old engravings. He wrote a history of the Christian Church down to our own ill-conducted Reformation, and composed a complete metrical version of the Psalms of David and of the Song of Solomon. These and many other productions, which he characterised as "The Employment of my Solitude," still remain in his own handwriting. Amongst them, Yorkshire men will hear with pleasure, is a "Treatise on the breeding of the Horse."

Of the quality of his wife we have already had a touch. She was one of the four daughters of Lord Vere of Tilbury, who came of a fine fighting family, and whose daughters had a roughish bringing-up, chiefly in the Netherlands. None of the daughters were reckoned beautiful, either in face or figure, and it may well be that Lady Fairfax had something about her of the old campaigner; but of her courage, sincerity, and goodness there can be no question. Her loyalty was no sickly fruit of "Church Principles," for her strong intelligence rejected scornfully the slavish doctrines, alien to our political constitution, of divine right and passive obedience; but a loyalty, none the less, it was, of a very valuable kind. She was fond of argument, and with Lady Fairfax at Nunappleton there was never likely to be any dearth of sensible talk and lively reminiscence. The tragedy of the 30th of January could never be forgotten, and it is possible that Marvell's most famous verses, so nobly descriptive of the demeanour of the king on that memorable occasion, derived their inspiration from discourse at Nunappleton.

Of the Lady Mary, aged twelve, we have no direct testimony. When she grew up and had her portrait painted she stands revealed as a stout young woman with a plain good-natured face. The poor soul needed all the good-nature heaven had bestowed upon her, for she had to bear the misery and disgrace which were the inevitable marriage-portion of the woman whose ill-luck it was to become the wife of George Villiers, second Duke of Buckingham. Somebody seems to have taught her philosophy, for she bore her misfortunes as best became a great lady, living as one who had sorrow but no grievance. The duke died in 1688; she lived on till 1704. She was ever a good friend to another ill-used solitary wife, Catherine of Braganza. Marvell had every reason to be proud of his pupil.

Beside the actual inmates of the great house, the whole countryside swarmed with Fairfaxes. At the Rectory of Bolton Percy was the late Lord-General's uncle, Henry Fairfax, and his two sons, Henry, who succeeded to the title, and the better-known Brian, the biographer of the Duke of Buckingham. At Stenton, four miles off, lived the widow of the gallant Sir William Fairfax, who died, covered with wounds, in 1644 before Montgomery Castle. There were two sons and two daughters at Stenton, whilst Charles Fairfax, another uncle, and the lawyer and genealogist of the family, lived at no great distance with no less than fourteen children. There were also sisters of Lord Fairfax, with families of their own, all settled in the same part of the county.

Such were the agreeable surroundings of our poet for two years, 1650-1652. I must leave it to the imaginations of my readers to fill up the picture, for excepting the poems, which we may safely assume were written at Nunappleton House, and—who can doubt it?—read aloud to its inmates, there is nothing more to be said.

Before considering the Nunappleton poetry, a word must be got in of bibliography. College exercises and complimentary verses excepted, Marvell printed none of his verse under his own name in his lifetime. So far as his themes were political there is no need to wonder at this. Indeed, the wonder is how, despite their anonymity, their author kept his ears; but why the Nunappleton verse should have remained in manuscript for more than thirty years is hard to explain.

Until Pope took his muse to market, poetry, apart from the drama, had no direct commercial value, or one too small to be ranked as a motive for publication. None the less, the age loved distinction and appreciated wit, and to be known as a poet whose verses "numbered good intellects" was to gain the *entrée* to the society of men both of intellect and fashion, and also, not infrequently, snug berths in the public service, and secretaryships to foreign missions and embassies. Thus there was always, in addition to natural vanity, a strong motive for a seventeenth-century poet to publish his poems. To-day one would hesitate to recommend a young man who wanted to get on in the world to publish a volume of verse; but the age of "wit" and "parts" is over.

It was not till 1681—three years after Marvell's death—that the small folio appeared with a fine portrait, still dear to the collector, which contains for the first time what may be called the "garden-poetry" of our author, together with some specimens of his political and satirical versification.

Marvell's most famous poem—*The Ode upon Cromwell's Return from Ireland*—is not included in the 1681 volume, and remained in manuscript until 1776, as also did the poem upon Cromwell's death.

The remainder of the political poems, which had made their first appearance as broadsheets, were reprinted after the Revolution in the well-known *Collection of Poems on Affairs of State*.[1] These verses were never owned by Marvell, and it is probable that some of them, though attributed to him, are not his at all. We have only tradition to go by. In the case of political satires, squibs, epigrams, rough popular occasional rhymes flung off both in haste and heat to be sold with old ballads in the market-place, we need not seek for better evidence than tradition, which indeed is often the only external evidence we have for the authorship of much more important things.

Now to return to the Nunappleton poetry.

In a poem of 776 lines Marvell tells the story and describes the charms of the house which Lord Fairfax built for himself during the war, and to which, as just narrated, he retired in the summer of 1650. The story is only too familiar a one, being writ large over many a fine property. Appleton House was Church loot. In the time of Henry, "the majestic lord that burst the bonds of Rome," the old house at Nunappleton was a Cistercian nunnery, a religious house. In 1542 the community was suppressed and its property appropriated by the great-grandfather of the Lord-General—one Sir Thomas Fairfax. The religious buildings were pulled down and a new secular house rose in their place. In these bare and sordid facts there is not much room for poetry, but there is a story thrown in. Shortly before 1518 a Yorkshire heiress, bearing the unromantic name of Isabella Thwaites, was living in the Cistercian abbey, under the guardianship of the abbess, the Lady Anna Langton. Property under the care of the Church is always supposed to be in danger, and the Lady Anna was freely credited with the desire to make a nun of her ward, and so keep her broad acres in Wharfedale and her messuages in York for the use of Mother Church. None the less, the young lady was allowed to go about and visit her neighbours, and whilst so doing she fell in love with Sir William Fairfax, or he fell in love with her or with her estates. Thereupon, so the story proceeds, the abbess kept her ward a close prisoner within the nunnery walls. Legal proceedings were taken, but in the end the privacy of the nunnery was invaded, and Miss Thwaites was abducted and married to Sir William Fairfax at the church of Bolton Percy. The lady abbess had to submit to *vis major*, but worse days were in front of her, for she lived on to see the nunnery itself despoiled, and the fair domains she had during a long life preserved and maintained for religious uses handed over to the son of her former ward, Isabella Thwaites.

Our poet begins by referring to the modest dimensions of the house, and the natural charms of its surroundings:—

"The house was built upon the place,
Only as for a mark of grace,
And for an inn to entertain
Its Lord awhile, but not remain.
Him Bishop's-hill or Denton may,
Or Billborow, better hold than they:
But Nature here hath been so free,
As if she said, 'Leave this to me.'
Art would more neatly have defac'd
What she had laid so sweetly waste
In fragrant gardens, shady woods,
Deep meadows, and transparent floods."

And then starts the story:—

"While, with slow eyes, we these survey,
And on each pleasant footstep stay,
 We opportunely may relate
The progress of this house's fate.
A nunnery first gave it birth,
(For virgin buildings oft brought forth)
And all that neighbour-ruin shows
The quarries whence this dwelling rose.
Near to this gloomy cloister's gates,
There dwelt the blooming virgin Thwaites,
Fair beyond measure, and an heir,
Which might deformity make fair;
And oft she spent the summer's suns
Discoursing with the subtle Nuns,
Whence, in these words, one to her weav'd,
As 'twere by chance, thoughts long conceiv'd:
'Within this holy leisure, we

Live innocently, as you see.
These walls restrain the world without,
But hedge our liberty about;
These bars inclose that wilder den
Of those wild creatures, callèd men,
The cloister outward shuts its gates,
And, from us, locks on them the grates.
Here we, in shining armour white,
Like virgin amazons do fight,
And our chaste lamps we hourly trim,
Lest the great Bridegroom find them dim.
Our orient breaths perfumèd are
With incense of incessant prayer;
And holy-water of our tears
Most strangely our complexion clears;
Not tears of grief, but such as those
With which calm pleasure overflows;
Or pity, when we look on you
That live without this happy vow.
How should we grieve that must be seen
Each one a spouse, and each a queen,
And can in heaven hence behold
Our brighter robes and crowns of gold!
When we have prayèd all our beads,
Some one the holy Legend reads,
While all the rest with needles paint
The face and graces of the Saint;
Some of your features, as we sewed,
Through every shrine should be bestowed,
And in one beauty we would take
Enough a thousand Saints to make.
And (for I dare not quench the fire
That me does for your good inspire)
'Twere sacrilege a man to admit
To holy things for heaven fit.
I see the angels in a crown
On you the lilies showering down;
And round about you glory breaks,
That something more than human speaks.
All beauty when at such a height,
Is so already consecrate.
Fairfax I know, and long ere this
Have marked the youth, and what he is;

But can he such a rival seem,
For whom you heaven should disesteem?
Ah, no! and 'twould more honour prove
He your devoto were than Love.
Here live belovèd and obeyed,
Each one your sister, each your maid,
And, if our rule seem strictly penned,
The rule itself to you shall bend.
Our Abbess, too, now far in age,
Doth your succession near presage.
How soft the yoke on us would lie,
Might such fair hands as yours it tie!
Your voice, the sweetest of the choir,
Shall draw heaven nearer, raise us higher,
And your example, if our head,
Will soon us to perfection lead.
Those virtues to us all so dear,
Will straight grow sanctity when here;
And that, once sprung, increase so fast,
Till miracles it work at last'"

What reply was given by the heiress to these arguments, and others of a still more seductive hue, the poet does not tell, but turns to the eager lover who asks, What should he do? He hints that a nunnery is no place for a virtuous maid, and that the nuns (unlike himself, I hope) are only thinking of her property. He complains that though the Court has authorised him to use either peace or force, the nuns still stand upon their guard.

"Ill-counselled women, do you know
Whom you resist or what you do?"

Using a most remarkable poetic licence, the poet refers to the fact that this barred-out lover is to be the progenitor of the great Lord Fairfax.

"Is not this he, whose offspring fierce
Shall fight through all the universe;
And with successive valour try
France, Poland, either Germany,
Till one, as long since prophesied,
His horse through conquered Britain ride?"

The lover determines to take the place by assault. It was not a very heroic enterprise, as Marvell describes it.

"Some to the breach, against their foes,
Their wooden Saints in vain oppose;
Another bolder, stands at push,
With their old holy-water brush,
While the disjointed Abbess threads
The jingling chain-shot of her beads;
But their loud'st cannon were their lungs,
And sharpest weapons were their tongues.
But waving these aside like flies,
Young Fairfax through the wall does rise.
Then the unfrequented vault appeared,
And superstition, vainly feared;
The relicks false were set to view;
Only the jewels there were true,
And truly bright and holy Thwaites,
That weeping at the altar waits.
But the glad youth away her bears,
And to the Nuns bequeathes her tears,
Who guiltily their prize bemoan,
Like gypsies who a child have stol'n."

The poet then goes on to glorify the results of this union and to describe happy days spent at Nunappleton by the descendants of Isabella Thwaites.

"At the demolishing, this seat
To Fairfax fell, as by escheat;
And what both nuns and founders willed,
'Tis likely better thus fulfilled.
For if the virgin proved not theirs,
The cloister yet remainèd hers;
Though many a nun there made her vow,
'Twas no religious house till now.
From that blest bed the hero came
Whom France and Poland yet does fame;
Who, when retirèd here to peace,
His warlike studies could not cease;
But laid these gardens out, in sport,
In the just figure of a fort,
And with five bastions it did fence,
As aiming one for every sense.
When in the east the morning ray
Hangs out the colours of the day,
The bee through these known alleys hums,

Beating the dian with its drums.
Then flowers their drowsy eyelids raise,
Their silken ensigns each displays,
And dries its pan, yet dank with dew,
And fills its flask with odours new.
These as their Governor goes by
In fragrant volleys they let fly,
And to salute their Governess
Again as great a charge they press:
None for the virgin nymph; for she
Seems with the flowers a flower to be.
And think so still! though not compare
With breath so sweet, or cheek so fair!
Well shot, ye firemen! Oh, how sweet
And round your equal fires do meet,
Whose shrill report no ear can tell,
But echoes to the eye and smell!
See how the flowers, as at parade,
Under their colours stand displayed;
Each regiment in order grows,
That of the tulip, pink and rose.
But when the vigilant patrol
Of stars walk round about the pole,
Their leaves, which to the stalks are curled,
Seem to their staves the ensigns furled.
Then in some flower's belovèd hut,
Each bee, as sentinel, is shut,
And sleeps so too, but, if once stirred,
She runs you through, nor asks the word.

Oh, thou, that dear and happy isle,
The garden of the world erewhile,
Thou Paradise of the four seas,
Which heaven planted us to please,
But, to exclude the world, did guard
With watery, if not flaming sword,—
What luckless apple did we taste,
To make us mortal, and thee waste?
Unhappy! shall we never more
That sweet militia restore,
When gardens only had their towers
And all the garrisons were flowers,
When roses only arms might bear,

And men did rosy garlands wear?
Tulips, in several colours barred,
Were then the Switzers of our guard;
The gardener had the soldier's place,
And his more gentle forts did trace;
The nursery of all things green
Was then the only magazine;
The winter quarters were the stoves,
Where he the tender plants removes.
But war all this doth overgrow:
We ordnance plant, and powder sow.

The arching boughs unite between
The columns of the temple green,
And underneath the wingèd quires
Echo about their tunèd fires.
The nightingale does here make choice
To sing the trials of her voice;
Low shrubs she sits in, and adorns
With music high the squatted thorns;
But highest oaks stoop down to hear,
And listening elders prick the ear;
The thorn, lest it should hurt her, draws
Within the skin its shrunken claws.
But I have for my music found
A sadder, yet more pleasing sound;
The stock-doves, whose fair necks are graced
With nuptial rings, their ensigns chaste,
Yet always, for some cause unknown,
Sad pair, unto the elms they moan.
O why should such a couple mourn,
That in so equal flames do burn!
Then as I careless on the bed
Of gelid strawberries do tread,
And through the hazels thick espy
The hatching throstle's shining eye,
The heron, from the ash's top,
The eldest of its young lets drop,
As if it stork-like did pretend
That tribute to its lord to send.

Thus I, easy philosopher,
Among the birds and trees confer;

And little now to make me, wants,
Or of the fowls, or of the plants;
Give me but wings as they, and I
Straight floating on the air shall fly;
Or turn me but, and you shall see
I was but an inverted tree.
Already I begin to call
In their most learn'd original,
And where I language want, my signs
The bird upon the bough divines,
And more attentive there doth sit
Than if she were with lime-twigs knit,
No leaf does tremble in the wind,
Which I returning cannot find.
One of these scattered Sibyls' leaves
Strange prophecies my fancy weaves,
And in one history consumes,
Like Mexique paintings, all the plumes;
What Rome, Greece, Palestine e'er said,
I in this light mosaic read.
Thrice happy he, who, not mistook,
Hath read in Nature's mystic book!
And see how chance's better wit
Could with a mask my studies hit!
The oak-leaves me embroider all,
Between which caterpillars crawl;
And ivy, with familiar trails,
Me licks and clasps, and curls and hales.
Under this Attic cope I move,
Like some great prelate of the grove;
Then, languishing with ease, I toss
On pallets swoln of velvet moss,
While the wind, cooling through the boughs,
Flatters with air my panting brows.
Thanks for your rest, ye mossy banks,
And unto you, cool zephyrs, thanks,
Who, as my hair, my thoughts too shed,
And winnow from the chaff my head!

How safe, methinks, and strong behind
These trees, have I encamped my mind,
Where beauty, aiming at the heart,
Bends in some tree its useless dart,

And where the world no certain shot
Can make, or me it toucheth not,
But I on it securely play
And gall its horsemen all the day.
Bind me, ye woodbines, in your twines
Curl me about, ye gadding vines,
And oh so close your circles lace,
That I may never leave this place!
But, lest your fetters prove too weak,
Ere I your silken bondage break,
Do you, O brambles, chain me too,
And, courteous briars, nail me through!

Oh what a pleasure 'tis to hedge
My temples here with heavy sedge,
Abandoning my lazy side,
Stretched as a bank unto the tide,
Or to suspend my sliding foot
On the osier's underminèd root,
And in its branches tough to hang,
While at my lines the fishes twang?
But now away, my hooks, my quills,
And angles, idle utensils!
The young MARIA walks to-night;

'Tis she that to these gardens gave
That wondrous beauty which they have;
She straightness on the woods bestows;
To her the meadow sweetness owes;
Nothing could make the river be
So crystal pure, but only she,
She yet more pure, sweet, straight, and fair
Than gardens, woods, meads, rivers are.

This 'tis to have been from the first
In a domestic heaven nursed,
Under the discipline severe
Of FAIRFAX, and the starry VERE;
Where not one object can come nigh
But pure, and spotless as the eye,
And goodness doth itself entail
On females, if there want a male."

This poem, having a biographical value, I have quoted at, perhaps, too great length. Other poems of this garden-period of Marvell's life are better known. His own English version of his Latin poem *Hortus* contains lovely stanzas:—

"How vainly men themselves amaze
To win the palm, the oak, or bays;
And their uncessant labours see
Crowned from some single herb or tree,
Whose short and narrow-vergèd shade
Does prudently their toils upbraid;
While all the flowers and trees do close,
To weave the garlands of Repose!

Fair Quiet, have I found thee here,
And Innocence, thy sister dear?
Mistaken long, I sought you then
In busy companies of men.
Your sacred plants, if here below,
Only among the plants will grow;
Society is all but rude
To this delicious solitude.

No white nor red was ever seen
So amorous as this lovely green.

What wond'rous life is this I lead!
Ripe apples drop about my head;
The luscious clusters of the vine
Upon my mouth do crush their wine;
The nectarine, and curious peach,
Into my hands themselves do reach;
Stumbling on melons, as I pass,
Insnared with flowers, I fall on grass.

Meanwhile the mind, from pleasure less,
Withdraws into its happiness;—
The mind, that ocean where each kind
Does straight its own resemblance find;—
Yet it creates, transcending these,
Far other worlds, and other seas,
Annihilating all that's made
To a green thought in a green shade."[1]

Well known as are Marvell's lines to his Coy Mistress, I have not the heart to omit them, so eminently characteristic are they of his style and humour:—

"Had we but world enough and time,
This coyness, lady, were no crime.
We would sit down and think which way
To walk, and pass our long love's day.
Thou by the Indian Ganges' side
Should'st rubies find: I by the tide
Of Humber would complain. I would
Love you ten years before the Flood,
And you should, if you please, refuse
Till the conversion of the Jews.
My vegetable love should grow
Vaster than empires and more slow.
An hundred years should go to praise
Thine eyes, and on thy forehead gaze;
Two hundred to adore each breast,
But thirty thousand to the rest;
An age at least to every part,
And the last age should show your heart.
For, lady, you deserve this state,
Nor would I love at lower rate.
 But at my back I always hear
Time's wingèd chariot hurrying near,
And yonder all before us lie
Deserts of vast eternity.
Thy beauty shall no more be found,
Nor in thy marble vault shall sound
My echoing song; then worms shall try
That long-preserved virginity,
And your quaint honour turn to dust,
And into ashes all my lust.
The grave's a fine and private place,
But none, I think, do there embrace.
Now, therefore, while the youthful hue
Sits on thy skin like morning dew,
And while thy willing soul transpires
At every pore with instant fires,
Now, let us sport us while we may;
And now, like amorous birds of prey,
Rather at once our time devour,
Than languish in his slow-chapt power!

Let us roll all our strength, and all
Our sweetness up into one ball;
And tear our pleasures with rough strife,
Through the iron gates of life!
Thus, though we cannot make our sun
Stand still, yet we will make him run."

Mr. Aitken's valuable edition of Marvell's poems and satires can now be had of all booksellers for two shillings,[1] and with these volumes in his possession the judicious reader will be able to supply his own reflections whilst life beneath the sun is still his. Poetry is a personal matter. The very canons of criticism are themselves literature. If we like the *Ars Poetica*, it is because we enjoy reading Horace.

[20:1] For an account of Flecknoe, see Southey's *Omniana*, i. 105. Lamb placed some fine lines of Flecknoe's at the beginning of the Essay *A Quakers' Meeting*.

[24:1] Grosart, vol. iii. p. 175.

[24:2] *See* preface to *Religio Laici*, Scott's *Dryden*, vol. x. p. 27.

[24:3] Jeremy Collier in his *Historical Dictionary* (1705) describes Marvell, to whom he allows more space (though it is but a few lines) than he does to Shakespeare, "as to his opinion he was a dissenter." In Collier's opinion Marvell may have been no better than a dissenter, but in fact he was a Churchman all his life, and it was Collier who lived to become a non-juror and a dissenter, and a schismatical bishop to boot.

[31:1] *Life of Lord Fairfax*, by C. R. Markham (1870), p. 365.

[35:1] The fifth edition is dated 1703.

[46:1] Many a reader has made his first acquaintance with Marvell on reading these lines in the *Essays of Elia* (*The Old Benchers of the Inner Temple*).

[47:1] *Poems and Satires of Andrew Marvell*, 2 vols. Routledge, 1905.

CHAPTER III

A CIVIL SERVANT IN THE TIME OF THE COMMONWEALTH

WHEN Andrew Marvell first made John Milton's acquaintance is not known. They must both have had common friends at or belonging to Cambridge. Fairfax may have made the two men known to each other, although it is just as likely that Milton introduced Marvell to Fairfax. All we know is that when the engagement at Nunappleton House came to an end, Marvell, being then minded to serve the State in some civil capacity, applied to the Secretary for Foreign Tongues for what would now be called a testimonial, which he was fortunate enough to obtain in the form of a letter to the Lord-President of the Council, John Bradshaw. Milton seems always to have liked Bradshaw, who was not generally popular even on his own side, and in the *Defensio Secunda pro populo Anglicano* extols his character and attainments in sonorous latinity. Bradshaw had become in February 1649 the first President of the new Council of State, which, after the disappearance of the king and the abolition of the House of Lords, took over the burden of the executive, and claimed the right to scrape men's consciences by administering to anybody it chose an oath requiring them to approve of what the House of Commons had done against the king, and of their abolition of kingly government and of the House of Peers, and that the legislative and supreme power was wholly in the House of Commons.

Before the creation of this Council the duties of Latin Secretary to the Parliament had been discharged by Georg Rudolph Weckherlin, a German diplomat who had married an Englishwoman. He retired in bad health at this time, and Milton was appointed to his place in 1649. When, later on, the sight of the most illustrious of all our civil servants failed him, Weckherlin returned to the office as Milton's assistant. In December 1652 ill-health again compelled Weckherlin's retirement.[1]

Milton's letter to Bradshaw, who had made his home at Eton, is dated February 21, 1653, and is as follows:—

"MY LORD,—But that it would be an interruption to the public wherein your studies are perpetually employed, I should now and then venture to supply thus my enforced absence with a line or two, though it were onely my business, and that would be no slight one, to make my due acknowledgments of your many favours; which I both do at this time and ever shall; and have this farther, which I thought my part to let you know of, that there will be with you to-morrow upon some occasion of business a gentleman whose name is Mr. Marvile, a man whom both by report and the converse I have had with him of singular desert for the State to make use of, who also offers himself, if there be any employment for him. His father was the Minister of

Hull, and he hath spent four years abroad in Holland, France, Italy, and Spain to very good purpose, as I believe, and the gaining of these four languages, besides he is a scholer and well-read in the Latin and Greek authors, and no doubt of an approved conversation, for he now comes lately out of the house of the Lord Fairfax, who was Generall, where he was intrusted to give some instructions in the languages to the Lady, his daughter. If upon the death of Mr. Weckerlyn the Councell shall think that I shall need any assistance in the performance of my place (though for my part I find no encumbrance of that which belongs to me, except it be in point of attendance at Conferences with Ambassadors, which I must confess in my condition I am not fit for) it would be hard for them to find a man so fit every way for that purpose as this gentleman: one who, I believe, in a short time would be able to do them as much service as Mr. Ascan. This, my Lord, I write sincerely without any other end than to perform my duty to the publick in helping them to an humble servant; laying aside those jealousies and that emulation which mine own condition might suggest to me by bringing in such a coadjutor; and remain, my Lord, your most obliged and faithful servant,

JOHN MILTON.

"*Feb. 21, 1652* (O.S.)."

Addressed: "For the Honourable the Lord Bradshawe."

No handsomer testimonial than this was ever penned. It was unsuccessful. When Milton wrote to Bradshaw, Weckherlin was in fact dead, and on his retirement in the previous December, John Thurloe, the very handy Secretary of the Council, had for the time assumed Weckherlin's duties, and obtained on that score an addition to his salary. No actual vacancy, therefore, occurred on Weckherlin's death. None the less, shortly afterwards, Philip Meadows, also a Cambridge man, was appointed Milton's assistant, and Marvell had to wait four years longer for his place.

When Marvell's connection with Eton first began is not to be ascertained. His friend, John Oxenbridge, who had been driven from his tutorship at Magdalen Hall, Oxford, by Laud in 1634 to

"Where the remote Bermudas ride,"

but had returned home, became in 1652 a Fellow of Eton College. Oliver St. John, who at this time was Chancellor of the University of Cambridge, and had married Oxenbridge's sister, was known to Marvell, and may have introduced him to his brother-in-law. At all events Marvell frequently visited Eton, where, however, he had the good sense to frequent not merely the cloisters, but the poor lodgings where the "ever memorable" John Hales, ejected from his fellowship, spent the last years of his life.

"I account it no small honour to have grown up into some part of his acquaintance and conversed awhile with the living remains of one of the clearest heads and best prepared breasts in Christendom."[1]

Hales died in 1656, and his *Golden Remains* were first published three years later. Marvell's words of panegyric are singularly well chosen. It is a curious commentary upon the confused times of the Civil War and Restoration that perhaps never before, and seldom, if ever, since, has England contained so many clear heads and well-prepared breasts as it did then. Small indeed is the influence of men of thought upon their immediate surroundings.

The Lord Bradshaw, we know, had a home in Eton, and on the occasion of one of Marvell's evidently frequent visits to the Oxenbridges, Milton entrusted him with a letter to Bradshaw and a presentation copy of the *Secunda defensio*. Marvell delivered both letter and book, and seems at once to have informed the distinguished author that he had done so. But alas for the vanity of the writing man! The sublime poet, who in his early manhood had composed *Lycidas*, and was in his old age to write *Paradise Lost*, demanded further and better particulars as to the precise manner in which the chief of his office received, not only the book, but the letter which accompanied it. Nobody is now left to think much of Bradshaw, but in 1654 he was an excellent representative of the class Carlyle was fond of describing as the *alors célèbre*. Prompted by this desire, Milton must have written to Marvell hinting, as he well knew how to do, his surprise at the curtness of his friend's former communication, and Marvell's reply to this letter has come down to us. It is Marvell's glory that long before *Paradise Lost* he recognised the essential greatness of the blind secretary, and his letter is a fine example of the mode of humouring a great man. Be it remembered, as we read, that this letter was not addressed to one of the greatest names in literature, but to a petulant and often peevish scholar, living of necessity in great retirement, whose name is never once mentioned by Clarendon, and about whom the voluminous Thurloe, who must have seen him hundreds of times, has nothing to say except that he was "a blind man who wrote Latin letters." Odder still, perhaps, Richard Baxter, whose history of his own life and times is one of the most informing books in the world, never so much as mentions the one and only man whose name can, without any violent sense of unfitness, be given to the age about which Baxter was writing so laboriously.

"HONOURED SIR,—I did not satisfie my self in the account I gave you of presentinge your Book to my Lord, although it seemed to me that I writ to you all which the messenger's speedy returne the same night from Eaton would permit me; and I perceive that, by reason of that hast, I did not give you satisfaction neither concerninge the delivery of your Letter at the same time. Be pleased therefore to pardon me and know that I tendered them both together. But my Lord read not the Letter while I was with him, which I attributed to our despatch, and some other businesse tendinge thereto, which I therefore wished ill to, so farr as it hindred an affaire much better and of greater importance, I mean that of reading your Letter. And to tell you truly mine own imagination, I thought that he would not open it while I was there, because he might suspect that I, delivering it just upon my departure, might have brought in it some second proposition like to that which you had before made to him by your Letter to my advantage. However, I assure myself that he has since read it, and you, that he did then witness all respecte to your person, and as much satisfaction concerninge your work as could be expected from so cursory a review and so sudden an account as he could then have of it from me. Mr. Oxenbridge, at his returne from London, will, I know, give you thanks for his book, as I do with all acknowledgement and humility for that you have sent me. I shall now studie it even to the getting of it by heart; esteeming it, according to my poore judgment (which yet I wish it were so right in all things else), as the most compendious scale for so much to the height of the Roman Eloquence, when I consider how equally it turnes and rises with so many figures it seems to me a Trajan's columne, in whose winding ascent we see imboss'd the severall monuments of your learned victoryes: And Salmatius and Morus make up as great a triumph as that of Decebalus, whom too, for ought I know, you shall have forced, as Trajan the other, to make themselves away out of a just desperation. I have an affectionate curiousity to know what becomes of Colonell Overton's businesse. And am exceeding glad that Mr. Skynner is got near you, the happinesse which I at the same time congratulate to him and envie, there being none who doth, if I may so say, more jealously honour you then, Honoured Sir, Your most affectionate humble servant,

ANDREW MARVELL.

"Eaton, *June 2, 1654.*"

Addressed: "For my most honoured friend,
John Milton, Esquire, Secretarye
for the Forrain affaires
at his house in Petty France,
Westminster."

To conclude Marvell's Eton experiences; in 1657, and very shortly before his obtaining his appointment as Milton's assistant in the place of Philip Meadows, who was sent on a mission to Lisbon, Marvell was chosen by the Lord-Protector to be tutor at Eton to Cromwell's ward, Mr. Dutton, and took up his residence with his pupil with the Oxenbridges. The following letter, addressed by Marvell to Oliver, will be read with interest:—

"May it please your Excellence,—It might, perhaps, seem fit for me to seek out words to give your Excellence thanks for myself. But, indeed, the only civility which it is proper for me to practice with so eminent a person is to obey you, and to perform honestly the work that you have set me about. Therefore I shall use the time that your Lordship is pleased to allow me for writing, onely for that purpose for which you have given me it; that is, to render you an account of Mr. Dutton. I have taken care to examine him several times in the presence of Mr. Oxenbridge, as those who weigh and tell over money before some witnesse ere they take charge of it; for I thought that there might be possibly some lightness in the coyn, or errour in the telling, which hereafter I should be bound to make good. Therefore, Mr. Oxenbridge is the best to make your Excellency an impartial relation thereof: I shall only say, that I shall strive according to my best understanding (that is, according to those rules your Lordship hath given me) to increase whatsoever talent he may have already. Truly, he is of gentle and waxen disposition; and God be praised, I cannot say he hath brought with him any evil impression; and I shall hope to set nothing into his spirit but what may be of a good sculpture. He hath in him two things that make youth most easy to be managed,—modesty, which is the bridle to vice; and emulation, which is the spur to virtue. And the care which your Excellence is pleased to take of him is no small encouragement and shall be so represented to him; but, above all, I shall labour to make him sensible of his duty to God; for then we begin to serve faithfully, when we consider He is our master. And in this, both he and I owe infinitely to your Lordship, for having placed us in so godly a family as that of Mr. Oxenbridge, whose doctrine and example are like a book and a map, not only instructing the ear, but demonstrating to the eye, which way we ought to travell; and Mrs. Oxenbridge has looked so well to him, that he hath already much mended his complexion; and now she is ordering his chamber, that he may delight to be in it as often as his studys require. For the rest, most of this time hath been spent in acquainting ourselves with him; and truly he is chearfull, and I hope thinks us to be good company. I shall, upon occasion, henceforward inform your Excellence of any particularities in our little affairs, for so I esteem it to be my duty. I have no more at present, but to give thanks to God for your Lordship, and to beg grace of Him, that I may approve myself, Your Excellency's most humble and faithful servant,

ANDREW MARVELL.

"Windsor, *July 28, 1653*.

"Mr. Dutton[1] presents his most humble service to your Excellence."

Something must now be said of Marvell's literary productions during this period, 1652-1657. It was in 1653 that he began his stormy career as an anonymous political poet and satirist. The Dutch were his first victims, good

Protestants though they were. Marvell never liked the Dutch, and had he lived to see the Revolution must have undergone some qualms.

In 1652 the Commonwealth was at war with the United Provinces. Trade jealousy made the war what politicians call "inevitable." This jealousy of the Dutch dates back to Elizabeth, and to the first stirring in the womb of time of the British navy. This may be readily perceived if we read Dr. John Dee's "Petty Navy Royal," 1577, and "A Politic Plat (plan) for the Honour of the Prince," 1580, and, somewhat later in date, "England's Way to Win Wealth," 1614.[1]

These short tracts make two things quite plain—first, the desire to get our share of the foreign fishing trade, then wholly in the hands of the Dutch; and second, the recognition that England was a sea-empire, dependent for its existence upon a great navy manned by the seafaring inhabitants of our coasts.

The enormous fishing trade done in our own waters by the Dutch, the splendid fleet of fishing craft with twenty thousand handy sailors on board, ready by every 1st of June to sail out of the Maas, the Texel, and the Vlie, to catch herring in the North Sea, excited admiration, envy, and almost despair.

"O, slothful England and careless countrymen! look but on these fellows that we call the plump Hollanders! Behold their diligence in fishing and our most careless negligence! Six hundred of these fisherships and more be great Busses, some six score tons, most of them be a hundred tons, and the rest three score tons and fifty tons; the biggest of them having four and twenty men, some twenty men, and some eighteen or sixteen men apiece. So there cannot be in this fleet of People no less than twenty thousand sailors.... No king upon the earth did ever see such a fleet of his own subjects at any time, and yet this fleet is there and then yearly to be seen. A most worthy sight it were, if they were my own countrymen, yet have I taken pleasure in being amongst them, to behold the neatness of their ships and fishermen, how every man knoweth his own place, and all labouring merrily together.[1]

"Now, in our sum of fishermen, let us see what vent have we for our fish in other countries, and what commodities and corn is brought into this Kingdom? And what ships are set in work by them whereby mariners are best employed. Not one. It is pitiful! ... This last year at Yarmouth there were three hundred idle men that could get nothing to do, living very poor for lack of employment, which most gladly would have gone to sea in Pinks if there had been any for them to go in.... And this last year the Hollanders did lade 12 sail of Holland ships with red herrings at Yarmouth for Civita Vecchia, Leghorn and Genoa and Marseilles and Toulon. Most of these being laden by the English merchants. So that if this be suffered the English owners of ships shall have but small employment for them."[2]

Nor was the other aspect of the case lost sight of. How can a great navy necessary for our sea-empire be manned otherwise than by a race of brave sea-faring men, accustomed from their infancy to handle boats?

"Fourthly, how many thousands of soldiers of all degrees would be by these means not only hardened well to brook all rage and disturbance of sea, but also would be well practised and trained to great perfection of understanding all manner of fight and service of sea, so that in time of great need that expert and hardy crew of some thousands of sea-soldiers would be to this realm a treasure incomparable.[1]

"We see the Hollanders being well fed in fishing affairs and stronger and lustier than the sailors who use the long Southern voyages, but these courageous, young, lusty, strong-fed younkers that shall be bred in the Busses, when His Majesty shall have occasion for their service in war against the enemy, will be fellows for the nonce! and will put more strength to an iron crow at a piece of great ordnance in training of a cannon, or culvining with the direction of the experimented master Gunner, then two or three of the forenamed surfeited sailors. And in distress of wind-grown sea and foul winter's weather, for flying forward to their labour, for pulling in a top-sail or a sprit-sail, or shaking off a bonnet in a dark night! for wet or cold cannot make them shrink nor stain, that the North Seas and the Busses and Pinks have dyed in the grain for such purposes."[2]

The years, as they went by, only served to increase English jealousy of the Dutch, who not only fished our water but did the carrying trade of the world. It was no rare sight to see Yarmouth full of Dutch bottoms, and Dutch sailors loading them with English goods.

In the early days of the Commonwealth the painfulness of the situation was accentuated by the fact that some of our colonies or plantations, as they were then called—Virginia and the Barbadoes, for example—stuck to the king and gave a commercial preference to the Dutch, shipping their produce to all parts of the world exclusively in Dutch bottoms. This was found intolerable, and in October 1651 the Long Parliament, nearing its violent end, passed the first Navigation Act, of which Ranke says: "Of all the acts ever passed in Parliament, it is perhaps the one which brought about the most important results for England and the world."[1]

The Navigation Act provided "that all goods from countries beyond Europe should be imported into England in English ships only; and all European goods either in English ships or in ships belonging to the countries from which these articles originally came."

This was a challenge indeed.

Another perpetual source of irritation was the Right of Search, that is, the right of stopping neutral ships and searching their cargoes for contraband. England asserted this right as against the Dutch, who, as the world's carriers, were most subject to the right, and not unnaturally denied its existence.

War was declared in 1652, and made the fame of two great admirals, Blake and Van Tromp. Oliver's spirit was felt on the seas, and before many months were over England had captured more than a thousand Dutch trading vessels, and brought business to a standstill in Amsterdam—then the great centre of commercial interests. When six short years afterwards the news of Cromwell's death reached that city, its inhabitants greatly rejoiced, crowding the streets and crying "the Devil is dead."

Andrew Marvell was impregnated with the new ideas about sea-power. A great reader and converser with the best intellects of his time, and a Hull man, he had probably early grasped the significance of Bacon's illuminating saying in the famous essay on the *True Greatness of Kingdoms and Estates* (first printed in 1612), "that he that commands the sea is at great liberty and may take as much and as little of the war as he will." Cromwell, though not the creator of our navy, was its strongest inspiration until Nelson, and no feature of his great administration so excited Marvell's patriotic admiration as the Lord-Protector's sleepless energy in securing and maintaining the command of the sea.

In Marvell's poem, first published as a broadsheet in 1655, entitled *The First Anniversary of the Government under His Highness the Lord-Protector*, he describes foreign princes soundly rating their ambassadors for having misinformed them as to the energies of the new Commonwealth:—

"'Is this,' saith one, 'the nation that we read
Spent with both wars, under a Captain dead!
Yet rig a navy while we dress us late
And ere we dine rase and rebuild a state?
What oaken forests, and what golden mines,
What mints of men—what union of designs!...
Needs must we all their tributaries be
Whose navies hold the sluices of the sea!
The ocean is the fountain of command,
But that once took, we captives are on land;
And those that have the waters for their share
Can quickly leave us neither earth nor air.'"

Marvell's aversion to the Dutch was first displayed in the rough lines called *The Character of Holland*, published in 1653 during the first Dutch War. As poetry the lines have no great merit; they do not even jingle agreeably—but they are full of the spirit of the time, and breathe forth that "envy, hatred, malice, and all uncharitableness" which are apt to be such large ingredients in the compound we call "patriotism." They begin thus:—

"Holland, that scarce deserves the name of land,
As but the off-scouring of the British sand,
And so much earth as was contributed
By English pilots when they heaved the lead,
Or what by the ocean's slow alluvion feel
Of shipwrecked cockle and the muscle-shell,—
This indigested vomit of the sea
Fell to the Dutch by just propriety."

The gallant struggle to secure their country from the sea is made the subject of curious banter:—

"How did they rivet with gigantic piles,
Thorough the centre their new-catched miles,
And to the stake a struggling country bound,
Where barking waves still bait the forced ground,
Building their watery Babel far more high,
To reach the sea, than those to scale the sky!
Yet still his claim the injured ocean laid,
And oft at leap-frog o'er their steeples played,
As if on purpose it on land had come
To show them what's their *mare liberum*.
A daily deluge over them does boil;
The earth and water play at level coil.
The fish ofttimes the burgher dispossessed,
And sat, not as a meat, but as a guest."

This final conceit greatly tickled the fancy of Charles Lamb, who was perhaps the first of the moderns to rediscover both the rare merits and the curiosities of our author. Hazlitt thought poorly of the jest.[1]

Marvell proceeds with his ridicule to attack the magistrates:—

"For, as with pygmies, who best kills the crane;
Among the hungry, he that treasures grain;
Among the blind, the one-eyed blinkard reigns;
So rules among the drowned, he that drains:
Not who first see the rising sun, commands,
But who could first discern the rising lands;
Who best could know to pump an earth so leak,

Him they their Lord, and Country's Father, speak;
To make a bank, was a great plot of state;
Invent a shovel, and be a magistrate."[1]

When the war-fever was raging such humour as this may well have passed muster with the crowd.

The incident—there is always an "incident"—which served as the actual excuse for hostilities, is referred to as follows:—

"Let this one courtesy witness all the rest,
When their whole navy they together pressed,
Not Christian captives to redeem from bands,
Or intercept the western golden sands,
No, but all ancient rights and leagues must fail,
Rather than to the English strike their sail;
To whom their weather-beaten province owes
Itself."

Two spirited lines describe the discomfiture of Van Tromp:—

"And the torn navy staggered with him home
While the sea laughed itself into a foam."

This first Dutch War came to an end in 1654, when Holland was compelled to acknowledge the supremacy of the English flag in the home waters, and to acquiesce in the Navigation Act. It is a curious commentary upon the black darkness that conceals the future, that Cromwell, dreading as he did the House of Orange and the youthful grandson of Charles the First, who at the appointed hour was destined to deal the House of Stuart a far deadlier stroke than Cromwell had been able to do, either on the field of battle or in front of Whitehall, refused to ratify the Treaty of Peace with the Dutch until John De Witt had obtained an Act excluding the Prince of Orange from ever filling the office of Stadtholder of the Province of Holland.

The contrast between the glory of Oliver's Dutch War and the shame of Charles the Second's sank deep into Marvell's heart, and lent bitterness to many of his later satirical lines.

Marvell's famous *Horatian Ode upon Cromwell's Return from Ireland* in 1650 has a curious bibliographical interest. So far as we can tell, it was first published in 1776. When it was composed we do not know. At Nunappleton House Oliver was not a *persona grata* in 1650, for he had no sooner come back from Ireland than he had stepped into the shoes of the Lord-General Fairfax; and there were those, Lady Fairfax, I doubt not, among the number, who believed that the new Lord-General thought it was high time he should be where Fairfax's "scruple" at last put him. We may be sure Cromwell's character was dissected even more than it was extolled at Nunappleton. The famous Ode is by no means a panegyric, and its true hero is the "Royal actor," whom Cromwell, so the poem suggests, lured to his doom. It is not likely that the Ode was composed after Marvell had left Nunappleton, though it may have been so before he went there. There is an old untraceable tradition that Marvell was among the crowd that saw the king die. What deaths have been witnessed, and with what strange apparent apathy, by the London crowd! But for this tradition one's imagination would trace to Lady Fairfax the most famous of the stanzas.

But to return to the history of the Ode. In 1776 Captain Edward Thompson, a connection of the Marvell family and a versatile sailor with a passion for print, which had taken some odd forms of expression, produced by subscription in three quarto volumes the first collected edition of Andrew Marvell's works, both verse and prose. Such an edition had been long premeditated by Thomas Hollis, one of the best friends literature had in the eighteenth century. It was Hollis who gave to Sidney Sussex College the finest portrait in existence of Oliver Cromwell. Hollis collected material for an edition of Marvell with the aid of Richard Barron, an early editor of Milton's prose works, and of Algernon Sidney's *Discourse concerning Government*. Barron, however, lost zeal as the task proceeded, and complained justly enough "of a want of anecdotes," and as the printer, the well-known and accomplished Bowyer, doubted the wisdom of the undertaking, it was allowed to drop. Barron died in 1766, and Hollis in 1774, but the collections made by the latter passed into the hands of Captain Thompson, who, with the assistance of Mr. Robert Nettleton, a grandson of one of Marvell's sisters, at once began to get his edition ready. On Nettleton's death his "Marvell" papers came into Thompson's hands, and among them was, to quote the captain's own words, "a volume of Mr. Marvell's poems, some written with his own hand and the rest copied by his order."

The *Horatian Ode* was in this volume, and was printed from it in Thompson's edition of 1776.

What has become of this manuscript book? It has disappeared—destroyed, so we are led to believe, in a fit of temper by the angry and uncritical sea-captain.

This precious volume undoubtedly contained some poems by Marvell, and as his handwriting was both well known from many examples, and is highly characteristic, we may also be certain that the captain was not mistaken in his assertion that some of these poems were in Marvell's own handwriting. But, as ill-luck would have it, the volume also contained poems written at a later period and in quite another hand. Among these latter pieces were Addison's verses, *The Spacious Firmament on High* and *When all thy Mercies, O my God*; Dr. Watts' paraphrase *When Israel freed from Pharaoh's Hand*; and Mallet's ballad *William and Margaret*. The two Addison pieces and the Watts paraphrase appeared for the first time in the *Spectator*, Nos. 453, 465, and 461, in 1712, and Mallet's ballad was first printed in 1724.

Still there these pieces were, in manuscript, in this volume, and as there were circumstances of mystification attendant upon their prior publication, what does the captain do but claim them all, *Songs of Zion* and sentimental ballad alike, as Marvell's. This of course brought the critics, ever anxious to air their erudition, down upon his head, raised his anger, and occasioned the destruction of the book.

Mr. Grosart says that Captain Thompson states that the *Horatian Ode* was in Marvell's handwriting. I cannot discover where this statement is made, though it is made of other poems in the volume, also published for the first time by the captain.

All, therefore, we know is that the Ode was first published in 1776 by an editor who says he found it copied in a book, subsequently destroyed, which contained (among other things) some poems written in Marvell's handwriting, and that this book was given to the editor by a grand-nephew of the poet.

Yet I imagine, poor as this evidence may seem to be, no student of Marvell's life and character (so far as his life reveals his character), and of his verse (so much of it as is positively known), wants more evidence to satisfy him that the *Horatian Ode* is as surely Marvell's as the lines upon *Appleton House*, the *Bermudas*, *To his Coy Mistress*, and *The Garden*.

The great popularity of this Ode undoubtedly rests on the three stanzas:—

"That thence the royal actor borne,
The tragic scaffold might adorn,
While round the armèd bands;
Did clap their bloody hands:

He nothing common did, or mean,
Upon that memorable scene,
But with his keener eye
The axe's edge did try;

Nor called the gods with vulgar spite
To vindicate his helpless right,

> But bowed his comely head
> Down, as upon a bed."

It is strange that the death of the king should be so nobly sung in an Ode bearing Cromwell's name and dedicate to his genius:—

> "So restless Cromwell could not cease
> In the inglorious arts of peace,
> But through adventurous war
> Urgèd his active star;
>
> ...
>
> Then burning through the air he went,
> And palaces and temples rent;
> And Cæsar's head at last
> Did through his laurels blast.
>
> 'Tis madness to resist or blame
> The force of angry Heaven's flame;
> And if we would speak true,
> Much to the man is due,
>
> Who, from his private gardens, where
> He lived reservèd and austere,
> (As if his highest plot
> To plant the bergamot),
>
> Could by industrious valour climb
> To ruin the great work of time,
> And cast the kingdoms old
> Into another mould."

The last stanzas of all have much pith and meaning in them:—

> "But thou, the war's and fortune's son,
> March indefatigably on!
> And for the last effect,
> Still keep the sword erect.
>
> Besides the force it has to fright
> The spirits of the shady night,

The same arts that did gain
A power, must it maintain."[1]

It is not surprising that this Ode was not published in 1650—if indeed it was the work of that, and not of a later year. There is nothing either of the courtier or of the partisan about its stately versification and sober, solemn thought. Entire self-possession, dignity, criticism of a great man and a strange career by one well entitled to criticise, are among the chief characteristics of this noble poem. It is infinitely refreshing, when reading and thinking about Cromwell, to get as far away as possible from the fanatic's scream and the fury of the bigot, whether of the school of Laud or Hobbes. Andrew Marvell knew Oliver Cromwell alive, and gazed on his features as he lay dead—he knew his ambition, his greatness, his power, and where that power lay. How much might we unwittingly have lost, if Captain Thompson had not printed a poem which for more than a century of years had remained unknown, and exposed to all the risks of a single manuscript copy!

When Cromwell sent his picture to Queen Christina of Sweden to commemorate the peace he concluded with her in 1654, Marvell, though not then attached to the public service, was employed to write the Latin couplet that accompanied the picture. He discharged his task as follows:—

In effigiem Oliveri Cromwell.

"Hæc est quæ toties inimicos umbra fugavit
At sub quâ cives otia lenta terunt."

The authorship of these lines is often attributed to Milton, but there is little doubt they are of Marvell's composition. They might easily have been better.

Marvell became Milton's assistant in September 1657, and the friendship between the two men was thus consolidated by the strong ties of a common duty. Milton's blindness making him unfit to attend the reception of foreign embassies, Marvell took his place and joined in respectfully greeting the Dutch ambassadors. After all he was but a junior clerk, still he doubtless rejoiced that his lines on Holland had been published anonymously. Literature was strongly represented in this department of State just then, for Cromwell's Chamberlain, Sir Gilbert Pickering, who represented Northamptonshire in Parliament, had taken occasion to introduce his nephew, John Dryden, to the public service, and he was attached to the same office as Andrew Marvell. Poets, like pigeons, have often taken shelter under our public roofs, but Milton, Marvell, and Dryden, all at the same time, form a remarkable constellation. Old Noll, we may be sure, had nothing to do with it. Marvell must have known Cromwell personally; but there is nothing to show that Milton and Cromwell ever met. The popular engraving which represents a theatrical Lord-Protector dictating despatches to a meek Milton is highly ludicrous. Cromwell could have as easily dictated a book of *Paradise Lost*, on the composition of which Milton began to be engaged during the last year of the Protectorate, as one of Milton's despatches.

In April 1657 Admiral Blake, the first great name in the annals of our navy, performed his last feat of arms by destroying the Spanish West Indian fleet at Santa Cruz without the loss of an English vessel. The gallant sailor died of fever on his way home, and was buried according to his deserts in the Abbey. His body, with that of his master, was by a vote of Parliament, December 4, 1660, taken from the grave and drawn to the gallows-tree, and there hanged and buried under it. Pepys, who was to know something of naval administration under the second Charles, has his reflections on this unpleasing incident.

Marvell's lines on Blake's victory over the Spaniards are not worthy of so glorious an occasion, but our great doings by land and sea have seldom been suitably recorded in verse. Drayton's *Song of Agincourt* is imperishable, but was composed nearly two centuries after the battle. The wail of Flodden Field still floats over the Border; but Miss Elliot's famous ballad was published in 1765. Even the Spanish Armada had to wait for Macaulay's spirited fragment. Mr. Addison's *Blenheim* stirred no man's blood; no poet sang Chatham's victories.[1] Campbell at a later day did better. We must be content with what we get.

Marvell's poem contains some vigorous lines, which show he was a good hater:—

"Now does Spain's fleet her spacious wings unfold,
Leaves the new world, and hastens for the old;
But though the wind was fair, they slowly swum,
Freighted with acted guilt, and guilt to come;
For this rich load, of which so proud they are,
Was raised by tyranny, and raised for war.......
For now upon the main themselves they saw
That boundless empire, where you give the law."

The Canary Islands are rapturously described—their delightful climate and their excellent wine. Obviously they should be annexed:—

"The best of lands should have the best of Kings."

The fight begins. "Bold Stayner leads" and "War turned the temperate to the torrid zone":—

"Fate these two fleets, between both worlds, had brought
Who fight, as if for both those worlds they fought.......
The all-seeing sun ne'er gazed on such a sight,
Two dreadful navies there at anchor fight,
And neither have, or power, or will, to fly;
There one must conquer, or there both must die."

Blake sinks the Spanish ships:—

"Their galleons sunk, their wealth the sea does fill,
The only place where it can cause no ill";

and the poet concludes:—

"Ah! would those treasures which both Indias have
Were buried in as large, and deep a grave!
War's chief support with them would buried be,
And the land owe her peace unto the sea.
Ages to come your conquering arms will bless.
There they destroyed what had destroyed their peace;
And in one war the present age may boast,
The certain seeds of many wars are lost."

Good politics, if but second-rate poetry. This was the last time the Spanish war-cry *Santiago, y cierra España* rang in hostility in English ears.

Turning for a moment from war to love, on the 19th of November 1657 Cromwell's third daughter, the Lady Mary Cromwell, was married to Viscount, afterwards Earl, Fauconberg. The Fauconbergs took revolutions calmly and, despite the disinterment of their great relative, accepted the Restoration gladly and lived to chuckle over the Revolution. The forgetfulness, no less than the vindictiveness, of men is often surprising. Marvell, who played the part of Laureate during the Protectorate, produced two songs for the conventionally joyful occasion. The second of the two is decidedly pretty for a November wedding:—

"*Hobbinol.* PHILLIS, TOMALIN, away!
Never such a merry day,
For the northern shepherd's son
Has MENALCAS' daughter won.

Phillis. Stay till I some flowers have tied
In a garland for the bride.

Tomalin. If thou would'st a garland bring,
PHILLIS, you may wait the spring:
They have chosen such an hour
When she is the only flower.

Phillis. Let's not then, at least, be seen
Without each a sprig of green.

Hobbinol. Fear not; at MENALCAS' hall
There are bays enough for all.
He, when young as we, did graze,
But when old he planted bays.

Tomalin. Here she comes; but with a look
Far more catching than my hook;
'Twas those eyes, I now dare swear,
Led our lambs we knew not where.

Hobbinol. Not our lambs' own fleeces are
Curled so lovely as her hair,
Nor our sheep new-washed can be
Half so white or sweet as she.

Phillis. He so looks as fit to keep
Somewhat else than silly sheep.

Hobbinol. Come, let's in some carol new
Pay to love and them their due.

All. Joy to that happy pair
Whose hopes united banish our despair.
What shepherd could for love pretend,
Whilst all the nymphs on Damon's choice attend?
What shepherdess could hope to wed
Before Marina's turn were sped?
Now lesser beauties may take place
And meaner virtues come in play;
While they
Looking from high
Shall grace
Our flocks and us with a propitious eye."

All this merriment came to an end on the 3rd of September 1658, when Oliver Cromwell died on the anniversary of Dunbar fight and of the field of Worcester. And yet the end, though it was to be sudden, did not at once seem likely to be so. There was time for the poets to tune their lyres. Waller, Dryden, Sprat, and Marvell had no doubt that "Tumbledown Dick" was to sit on the throne of his father and "still keep the sword erect," and were ready with their verses.

Westminster Abbey has never witnessed a statelier, costlier funeral than that of "the late man who made himself to be called Protector," to quote words from one of the most impressive passages in English prose, the opening sentences of Cowley's *Discourse by way of Vision concerning the Government of Oliver Cromwell*. The representatives of kings, potentates, and powers crowded the aisles, and all was done that pomp and ceremony could do. Marvell, arrayed in the six yards of mourning the Council had voted him on the 7th of September, was, we may be sure, in the Abbey, and it may well be that his blind colleague, to whom the same liberal allowance had been made, leant on his arm during the service. Milton's muse remained silent. The vote of the House of Commons ordering the undoing of this great ceremony was little more than two years ahead. O *caeca mens hominum!*

Among the poems first printed by Captain Thompson from the old manuscript book was one which was written therein in Marvell's own hand entitled "A poem upon the Death of his late Highness the Protector." Its composition was evidently not long delayed:—

"We find already what those omens mean,
Earth ne'er more glad nor Heaven more serene.
Cease now our griefs, calm peace succeeds a war,
Rainbows to storms, Richard to Oliver."

The lines best worth remembering in the poem are the following:—

"I saw him dead: a leaden slumber lies,
And mortal sleep over those wakeful eyes;
Those gentle rays under the lids were fled,
Which through his looks that piercing sweetness shed;
That port, which so majestic was and strong,
Loose, and deprived of vigour, stretched along;
All withered, all discoloured, pale and wan,
How much another thing, no more that man!
O, human glory vain! O, Death! O, wings!
O, worthless world! O, transitory things!
Yet dwelt that greatness in his shape decayed,

That still though dead, greater than Death he laid,
And in his altered face you something feign
That threatens Death, he yet will live again."

[49:1] In 1659 Clarendon, then Sir Edward Hyde, and in Brussels, writing to Sir Richard Fanshaw, says, "You are the secretary of the Latin tongue and I will mend the warrant you sent, and have it despatched as soon as I hear again from you, but I must tell you the place in itself, if it be not dignified by the person who hath some other qualification, is not to be valued. There is no signet belongs to it, which can be only kept by a Secretary of State, from whom the Latin Secretary always receives orders and prepares no despatches without his direction, and hath only a fee of a hundred pound a year. And therefore, except it hath been in the hands of a person who hath had some other employment, it hath fallen to the fortune of inconsiderable men as Weckerlin was the last" (*Hist. MSS. Com., Heathcote Papers*, 1899, p. 9).

[51:1] *The Rehearsal Transprosed.*—Grosart, iii. 126.

[55:1] Even Mr. Firth can tell me nothing about this Ward of Cromwell's.

[56:1] For reprints of these tracts, see *Social England Illustrated*, Constable and Co., 1903.

[57:1] "England's Way to Win Wealth." See *Social England Illustrated*, p. 253.

[57:2] *Ibid.* p. 265.

[58:1] Dr. Dee's "Petty Navy Royal." *Social England Illustrated*, p. 46.

[58:2] "England's Way to Win Wealth." *Social England Illustrated*, p. 268.

[59:1] Ranke's *History of England during the Seventeenth Century*, vol. iii. p. 68.

[61:1] See Leigh Hunt's *Wit and Humour* (1846), pp. 38, 237.

[62:1] Butler's lines, *A Description of Holland*, are very like Marvell's:—

"A Country that draws fifty foot of water
In which men live as in a hold of nature.......
They dwell in ships, like swarms of rats, and prey
Upon the goods all nations' fleets convey;......
That feed like cannibals on other fishes,
And serve their cousin-germans up in dishes:
A land that rides at anchor and is moor'd,
In which they do not live but go aboard."

Marvell and Butler were rival wits, but Holland was a common butt; so powerful a motive is trade jealousy.

^{67:1} "To one unacquainted with Horace, this Ode, not perhaps so perfect as his are in form, and with occasional obscurities of expression, which Horace would not have left, will give a truer notion of the kind of greatness which he achieved than could, so far as I know, be obtained from any other poem in our language."—*Dean Trench*.

^{70:1} "In the last war, when France was disgraced and overpowered in every quarter of the globe, when Spain coming to her assistance only shared her calamities, and the name of an Englishman was reverenced through Europe, no poet was heard amidst the general acclamation; the fame of our counsellors and heroes was entrusted to the gazetteer."—Dr. Johnson's *Life of Prior*.

CHAPTER IV

IN THE HOUSE OF COMMONS

CROMWELL'S death was an epoch in Marvell's history. Up to that date he had, since he left the University, led the life of a scholar, with a turn for business, and was known to many as an agreeable companion and a lively wit. He was keenly interested in public affairs, and personally acquainted with some men in great place, and for a year before Cromwell's death he had been in a branch of the Civil Service; but of the wear and tear, the strife and contention, of what are called "practical politics" he knew nothing from personal experience.

Within a year of the Protector's death all this was changed and, for the rest of his days, with but the shortest of occasional intervals, Andrew Marvell led the life of an active, eager member of Parliament, knowing all that was going on in the Chamber and hearing of everything that was alleged to be going on in the Court; busily occupied with the affairs of his constituents in Hull, and daily watching, with an increasingly heavy heart and a bitter humour, the corruption of the times, the declension of our sea-power, the growing shame of England, and what he believed to be a dangerous conspiracy afoot for the undoing of the Reformation and the destruction of the Constitution in both Church and State.

"Garden-poetry" could not be reared on such a soil as this. The age of Cromwell and Blake was over. The remainder of Marvell's life (save so far as personal friendship sweetened it) was spent in politics, public business, in concocting roughly rhymed and bitter satirical poems, and in the composition of prose pamphlets.

Through it all Marvell remained very much the man of letters, though one with a great natural aptitude for business. His was always the critical attitude. He was the friend of Milton and Harrington, of the political philosophers who invented paper constitutions in the "Rota" Club, and of the new race of men whose thoughts turned to Natural Science, and who founded the Royal Society. Office he never thought of. He could have had it had he chosen, for he was a man of mark, even of distinction, from the first. Clarendon has told us how members of the House of Commons "got on" in the Long Parliament of Charles the Second. It was full of the king's friends, who ran out of the House to tell their shrewd master the gossip of the lobbies, "commended this man and discommended another who deserved better, and would many times, when His Majesty spoke well of any man, ask His Majesty if he would give them leave to let that person know how gracious His Majesty was to him, or bring him to kiss his hand. To which he commonly consenting, every one of his servants delivered some message from him to a

Parliament man, and invited him to Court, as if the King would be willing to see him. And by this means the rooms at Court were always full of the members of the House of Commons. This man brought to kiss his hand, and the King induced to confer with that man and to thank him for his affection, which could never conclude without some general expression of grace or promise, which the poor gentleman always interpreted to his own advantage, and expected some fruit from it that it could never yield."

The suspicious Clarendon, already shaking to his fall, goes on to add, "all which, being contrary to all former order, did the King no good, and rendered those unable to do him service who were inclined to it."[1]

It is a lifelike picture Clarendon draws of the crowded rooms, and of the witty king moving about fooling vanity, ambition, and corruption to the top of their bent. That the king chose his own ministers is plain enough.

Marvell was at the beginning well disposed towards Charles. They had some points in common; and among them a quick sense of humour and a turn for business. But the member for Hull must soon have recognised that there was no place for an honest quick-witted man in any Stuart administration.

Marvell and his great chief remained in their offices until the close of the year 1659, when the impending Restoration enforced their retirement. Milton used his leisure to pour forth excited tracts to prove how easy it would still be to establish a Free Commonwealth. Once again, and for the last time, he prompted the age to quit its clogs

"by the known rules of ancient liberty."

These pamphlets of Milton's prove how little that solitary thinker ever knew of the real mind and temper of the English people.

The Lord Richard Cromwell was exactly the sort of eldest son a great soldier like Oliver, who had put his foot on fortune's neck, was likely to have. Richard (1626-1712) was not, indeed, born in the purple, but his early manhood was nurtured in it. Religion, as represented by long sermons, tiresome treatises, and prayerful exercises, bored him to death. Of enthusiasm he had not a trace, nor was he bred to arms. He delighted in hunting, in the open air, and the company of sportsmen. Whatever came his way easily, and as a matter of right, he was well content to take. He bore himself well on State occasions, and could make a better speech than ever his father was able to do. But he was not a "restless" Cromwell, and had no faith in his destiny. I do not know whether he had ever read *Don Quixote*, in Shelton's translation, a very popular book of the time; probably not, for, though Chancellor of the University of Oxford, Richard was not a reading man, but if he had, he must have sympathised with Sancho Panza's attitude of mind towards the famous island.

"If your highness has no mind that the government you promised should be given me, God made me of less, and perhaps it may be easier for Sancho, the Squire, to get to Heaven than for Sancho, the Governor. *In the dark all cats are gray.*"

The new Protector took up the reins of power with proper forms and ceremonies, and at once proceeded to summon a Parliament, an Imperial Cromwellian Parliament, containing representatives both from Scotland and Ireland. In this Parliament Andrew Marvell sat for the first time as one of the two members for Kingston-upon-Hull. His election took place on the 10th of January 1659, being the first county day after the sheriff had received the writ. Five candidates were nominated: Thomas Strickland, Andrew Marvell, John Ramsden, Henry Smyth, and Sir Henry Vane, and a vote being taken in the presence of the mayor, aldermen, and many of the burgesses, John Ramsden and Andrew Marvell were declared duly elected.

Nobody to-day, glancing his eye over a list of the knights and burgesses who made up Richard Cromwell's first and last Parliament, would ever guess that it represented an order of things of the most recent date which was just about to disappear. On paper it has a solid look. The fine old crusted Parliamentary names with which the clerks were to remain so long familiar as the members trooped out to divide were more than well represented.[1] The Drakes of Amersham were there; Boscawens, Bullers, and Trelawneys flocked from Cornwall; Sir Wilfred Lawson sat for Cumberland, and his son for Cockermouth; a Knightly represented Northamptonshire, whilst Lucys from Charlecote looked after Warwick, both town and county. Arthur Onslow came from Surrey, a Townshend from Norfolk, and, of course, a Bankes from Corfe Castle;[2] Oxford University, contented, as she occasionally is, to be represented by a great man, had chosen Sir Matthew Hale, whilst the no less useful and laborious Thurloe sat for the sister University. Anthony Ashley Cooper was there, but in opposition, snuffing the morrow. Mildmays, Lawleys, Binghams, Herberts, Pelhams, all travelled up to London with the Lord-Protector's writs in their pockets. A less revolutionary assembly never met, though there was a regicide or two among them. But when the members found themselves alone together there was some loose talk.

On the 27th of January 1659 Marvell attended for the first time in his place, when the new Protector opened Parliament, and made a speech in the House of Lords, which was pronounced at the time to be "a very handsome oration."

The first business of the Commons was to elect a Speaker, nor was their choice a very lucky one, for it first fell on Chaloner Chute, who speedily breaking down in health, the Recorder of London was appointed his substitute, but the Recorder being on his deathbed at the time, and Chute dying very shortly afterwards, Thomas Bampfield was elected Speaker, and continued so to be until the Parliament was dissolved by proclamation on the 22nd of April. This proclamation was Richard Cromwell's last act of State.

Marvell's first Parliament was both short and inglorious. One only of its resolutions is worth quoting:—

"That a very considerable navy be forthwith provided, and put to sea for the safety of the Commonwealth and the preservation of the trade and commerce thereof."

It was, however, the army and not the navy that had to be reckoned with—an army unpaid, angry, suspicious, and happily divided. I must not trace the history of faction. There is no less exalted page in English history since the days of Stephen. Monk is its fitting hero, and Charles the Second its expensive saviour of society. The story how the Restoration was engineered by General Monk, who, if vulgar, was adroit, both on land and sea, is best told from Monk's point of view in the concluding chapter of *Baker's Chronicle* (Sir Roger de Coverley's favourite Sunday reading), whilst that old-fashioned remnant, who still love to read history for fun, may not object to be told that they will find printed in the Report of the Leyborne-Popham Papers (*Historical Manuscripts Commission*, 1899, p. 204) a *Narrative of the Restoration*, by Mr. John Collins, the Chief Butler of the Inner Temple, proving in great and highly diverting detail how this remarkable event was really the work not so much of Monk as of the Chief Butler.

Richard Cromwell having slipped the collar, the officers assumed command, as they were only too ready to do, and recalled the old, dishonoured, but pertinacious Rump Parliament, which, though mustering at first but forty-two members, at once began to talk and keep journals as if nothing had happened since the day ten years before, when it was sent about its business. Old Speaker Lenthall was routed out of obscurity, and much against his will, and despite his protests, clapped once more into the chair. Dr. John Owen, an old parliamentary preaching hand, was once again requisitioned to preach before the House, which he did at enormous length one fine Sunday in May.

The Rump did not prove a popular favourite. It was worse than Old Noll himself, who could at least thrash both Dutchman and Spaniard, and be even more feared abroad than he was hated at home. The City of London, then almost an Estate of the Realm, declared for a Free Parliament, and it soon became apparent to every one that the whole country was eager to return as soon as possible to the old mould. Nothing now stood between Charles and his own but half a dozen fierce old soldiers and their dubious, discontented, unpaid men.

It was once commonly supposed (it is so no longer), that the Restoration party was exclusively composed of dispossessed Cavaliers, bishops in hiding, ejected parsons, high-flying *jure divino* Episcopalians, talkative toss-pots, and the great pleasure-loving crowd, cruelly repressed under the rule of the saints. Had it been left to these ragged regiments, the issue would have been doubtful, and the result very different. The Presbyterian ministers who occupied the rectories and vicarages of the Church of England and their well-to-do flocks in both town and country were, with but few exceptions, all for King Charles and a restored monarchy. In this the ministers may have shown a sound political instinct, for none of them had any more mind than the Anglican bishops to tolerate Papists, Socinians, Quakers, and Fifth Monarchy men, but in their management of the business of the Restoration these divines exposed themselves to the same condemnation that Clarendon in an often-quoted passage passed upon his own clerical allies. When read by the light of the Act of "Uniformity," the "Corporation," the "Five Mile," and the "Conventicle" Acts, the conduct of the Presbyterians seems recklessness itself, whilst the ignorance their ministers displayed of the temper of the people they had lived amongst all their lives, and whom they adjured to cry *God save the King*, but not to drink his Majesty's health (because health-drinking was forbidden in the Old Testament), would be startling were it not so eminently characteristic.[1]

The Rump, amidst the ridicule and contempt of the populace, was again expelled by military force on the 13th of October 1659. The officers were divided in opinion, some supporting, others, headed by Lambert, opposing the Parliament; but *vis major*, or superior cunning, was on the side of Lambert, who placed his soldiers in the streets leading to Westminster Hall, and when the Speaker came in his coach, his horses were turned, and he was conducted very civilly home. The regiments that should have resisted, "observing that they were exposed to derision," peaceably returned to their quarters.

Monk, in the meanwhile, was advancing with his army from Edinburgh, and affected not to approve of the force put upon Parliament. The feeling for a Free Parliament increased in strength and violence every day. The Rump was for a third time restored in December by the section of the London army that supported its claim. Lenthall was once more in the chair, and the journals were resumed without the least notice of past occurrences. Monk, having reached London amidst great excitement, went down to the House and delivered an ambiguous speech. Up to the last Monk seems to have remained uncertain what to do. The temper of the City, which was fiercely anti-Rump, may have decided him. At all events he invited the secluded, that is the expelled, members of the old Long Parliament to take their seats along with the others, and in a formal declaration addressed to Parliament, dated the 21st of February 1660, he counselled it among other things to dissolve legally "in order to make way for a succession of Parliaments." In a word, Monk declared for a Free Parliament. Great indeed were the national rejoicings.

On the 16th of March 1660 a Bill was read a third time dissolving the Parliament begun and holden at Westminster, 3rd November 1640, and for the calling and holding of a Parliament at Westminster on the 25th of April 1660. This time an end was really made of the Rump, though for many a long day there were parliamentary pedants to be found in the land ready to maintain that the Long Parliament had never been legally dissolved and still *de jure* existed; so long, I presume, as any single member of it remained alive.

Marvell was not a "Rumper," but on the 2nd of April 1660 he was again elected for Hull to sit in what is usually called the Convention Parliament. John Ramsden was returned at the head of the poll with 227 votes, Marvell receiving 141. There were four defeated candidates.

With this Convention Parliament begins Marvell's remarkable correspondence, on fine folio sheets of paper, with the corporation of Hull, whose faithful servant he remained until death parted them in 1678.

This correspondence, which if we include in it, as we well may, the letters to the Worshipful Society of Masters and Pilots of the Trinity House in Hull, numbers upwards of 350 letters, and with but one considerable gap (from July 1663 to October 1665) covers the whole period of Marvell's membership, is, I believe, unique in our public records. The letters are preserved at Hull, where I hope care is taken to preserve them from the autograph hunter and the autograph thief. Captain Thompson printed a great part of this correspondence in 1776, and Mr. Grosart gave the world the whole of it in the second volume of his edition of Marvell's complete works.

An admission may as well be made at once. This correspondence is not so interesting as it might have been expected to prove. Marvell did not write letters for his biographer, nor to instruct posterity, nor to serve any party purpose, nor even to exhibit honest emotion, but simply to tell his employers, whose wages he took, what was happening at Westminster. He kept his reflections either to himself or for his political broadsheets, and indeed they were seldom of the kind it would have been safe to entrust to the post.

Good Mr. Grosart fusses and frets terribly over Marvell's astonishing capacity for chronicling in sombre silence every kind of legislative abomination. It is at times a little hard to understand it, for Hull was what may be called a Puritan place. No doubt caution dictated some of the reticence—but the reserve of Marvell's character is one of the few traits of his personality that has survived. He was a satirist, not an enthusiast.

I will give the first letter *in extenso* to serve as a specimen, and a very favourable one, of the whole correspondence:—

"*Nov. 17, 1660.*

"GENTLEMEN, MY WORTHY FRIENDS,—Although during the necessary absence of my partner, Mr. Ramsden, I write with but halfe a penn, and can scarce perswade myselfe to send you so imperfect an account of your own and the publick affairs, as I needs must for want of his assistance; yet I had rather expose mine own defects to your good interpretation, then excuse thereby a totall neglect of my duty, and that trust which is divided upon me. At my late absence out of Town I had taken such order that if you had commanded me any thing, I might soon haue received it, and so returned on purpose to this place to haue obeyed you. But hearing nothing of that nature howeuer, I was present the first day of the Parliament's sitting, and tooke care to write to Mr. Maior what work we had cut out. Since when, we have had little new, but onely been making a progresse in those things I then mentioned. There is yet brought in an Act in which of all others your corporation is the least concerned: that is, where wives shall refuse to cohabit with their husbands, that in such case the husband shall not be liable to pay any debts which she may run into, for clothing, diet, lodging, or other expenses. I wish with all my heart you were no more touched in a vote that we haue made for bringing in an Act of a new Assessment for six moneths, of 70,000li. *per mensem*, to begin next January. The truth is, the delay ere monyes can be got in, eats up a great part of all that is levying, and that growing charge of the Army and Navy doubles upon us. And that is all that can be said for excuse of ourselues to the Country, to whom we had giuen our own hopes of no further sessment to be raised, but must now needs incurre the censure of improvidence before or prodigality now, though it becomes no private member, the resolution having passed the House, to interpose further his own judgment in a thing that can not be remedied; and it will be each man's ingenuity not to grudge an after-payment for that settlement and freedome from Armyes and Navyes, which before he would haue been glad to purchase with his whole fortune. There remain some eight Regiments to be disbanded, but those all horse in a manner, and some seauenteen shipps to be payd of, that haue laid so long upon charge in the harbour, beside fourscore shipps which are reckoned to us for this Winter guard. But after that, all things are to go upon his Majestye's own purse out of the Tunnage and Poundage and his other revenues. But there being so great a provision made for mony, I doubt not but ere we rise, to see the whole army disbanded, and according to the Act, hope to see your Town once more ungarrisond, in which I should be glad and happy to be instrumentall to the uttermost. For I can not but remember, though then a child, those blessed days when the youth of your own town were trained for your militia, and did, methought, become their arms much better than any soldiers that I haue seen there since. And it will not be amisse if you please (now that we are about a new Act of regulating the Militia, that it may be as a standing strength, but not as ill as a perpetuall Army to the Nation) to signify to me any thing in that matter that were according to your ancient custome and desirable for you. For though I can promise little, yet I intend all things for your service. The Act for review of the Poll bill proceeds, and that for making this Declaration of his Majesty a Law in religious matters. Order likewise is giuen for drawing up all the votes made during our last sitting, in the businesse of Sales of Bishops' and Deans' and Chapters' lands into an Act, which I should be glad to see passed. The purchasers the other day offerd the house 600,000li. in ready mony, and to make the Bishops', etc., revenue as good or better then before. But the House thought it not fit or seasonable to hearken to it. We are so much the more concernd to see that great interest of the purchasers satisfyed and quieted, at least in that way which our own votes haue propounded. On Munday next we are to return to the consideration of apportioning 100,000li. per annum upon all the lands in the nation, in lieu of the Court of Wards. The debate among the Countyes, each thinking it self overrated, makes the successe of that businesse something casuall, and truly I shall not assist it much for my part, for it is little reason that your Town should contribute in that charge. The Excise bill for longer continuance (I wish it proue not too long) will come in also next weeke. And I foresee we shall be called upon shortly to effect our vote made the former sitting, of raising his Majestie's revenue to 1,200,000li. per Annum. I do not love to write so much of this mony news. But I think you haue observed that Parliaments have been always made use of to that purpose, and though we may buy gold too deare, yet we must at any rate be glad of Peace, Freedom, and a good Conscience. Mr. Maior tells me, your duplicates of the Poll are coming up. I shall go with them to the Exchequer and make your excuse, if any be requisite. My long silence hath made me now trespasse on the other hand in a long letter, but I doubt not of your good construction of so much familiarity and trouble from, Gentlemen, your most affectionate friend and servant,

"ANDR: MARVELL.

"WESTMINSTER, *Nov. 17, 1660.*"

Although this first letter of the Hull correspondence is dated the 17th of November 1660, the Convention Parliament began its sittings on the 25th of April.

In composition this Convention Parliament was very like Richard Cromwell's, and indeed it contained many of the same members, whose loyalty, however, was less restrained than in 1659. All the world knew what brought this Parliament together. It was to make the nation's peace with its king, either on terms or without terms. "We are all Royalists now" are words which must often have been on the lips of the members of this House. One can imagine the smiles, half grim, half ironical, that would accompany their utterance. Such a right-about-face could never be dignified. It is impossible not to be reminded of schoolboys at the inevitable end of "a barring out." The sarcastic comment of Clarendon has not lost its sting. "From this time there was such an emulation and impatience in Lords, Commons, and City, and generally over the Kingdom, who should make the most lively expressions of their duty and of their joy, that a man could not but wonder where those people dwelt who had done all the mischief and kept the King so many years from enjoying the comfort and support of such excellent subjects."[1]

The most significant sentence in Marvell's first letter to his constituents is that in which he refers to the Bill for making Charles's declaration in religious matters the law of the land. Had the passing of any such Bill been possible, how different the history of England would have been!

The declaration Marvell is referring to was contained in the famous message from Breda, which was addressed by Charles to all his loving subjects of what degree or quality, and was expressed as follows:—

"And because the passion and uncharitableness of the times have produced several opinions in Religion by which men are engaged in parties and animosities against each other (which, when they shall hereafter unite in a freedom of conversation, will be composed or better understood) we do declare a liberty to tender Consciences, and that no man shall be disquieted or called in question for differences of opinion in matters of Religion which do not disturb the peace of the Kingdom; and that we shall be ready to consent to such an Act of Parliament as upon mature deliberation shall be offered to us for the full granting of that indulgence."

It is only doing the king bare justice to say that he was always ready and willing to keep this part of his royal word—but it proved an impossibility.

A Roman Catholic as a matter of creed, a Hobbist in conversation, a sensualist in practice, and the shrewdest though most indolent of cynics in council, Charles, in this matter of religious toleration, would gladly have kept his word, not indeed because it was his word, for on the point of honour he was indifferent, but because it jumped with his humour, and would have mitigated the hard lot of the Catholics. Charles was not a theorist, all his tastes being eminently practical, not to say scientific. He was not a tyrant, but a *de facto* man from head to heel. For the *jure divino* of the English Episcopate he cared as little as Oliver had ever done for the *jure divino* of the English Crown. Oliver once said, and he was not given to *braggadocio*, that he would fire his pistol at the king "as soon as at another if he met him in battle," and the second Charles would have thought no more of beheading an Anglican bishop than he did of sending Sir Harry Vane to the scaffold. Honesty and virtue, on the rare occasions Charles encountered them, he admired much as a painter admires the colours of a fine sunset. Above everything else Charles was determined never again, if he could help it, to be sent on his travels, to be snubbed and starved in foreign courts.

Sir Thomas Urquhart of Cromartie, the first and best translator of Rabelais, is said to have died of laughing on hearing of the Restoration; Charles did not die, but he must have laughed inwardly at the spectacle that met his eyes everywhere as he made his often-described progress from Dover to London, and examined the gorgeous beds and quilts, fine linen and carpets, couches, horses and liveries, his faithful Commons had been at the pains and at the expense of providing for his comfort.

A few years afterwards Marvell wrote the following lines:—

"Of a tall stature and of sable hue,
Much like the son of Kish, that lofty Jew;
Twelve years complete he suffered in exile
And kept his father's asses all the while.
At length, by wonderful impulse of fate,
The people called him home to help the state,
And what is more they sent him money too
To clothe him all from head to foot anew;
Nor did he such small favours then disdain,
Who in his thirtieth year began his reign."[1]

The "small favours" grew in size year by year.

Why it was impossible for Charles to keep his word may be read in Clarendon's *Life*, and in the history of the Savoy Conference, and need not be restated here. In the opinion of the Anglican clergy, the king's divine right stood no higher than their own. They too had suffered in exile. They had been "robbed" of their tithes, and turned out of their palaces, rectories and vicarages, and excluded from the churches they still called "theirs." Their Book of Common Prayer was no longer in common use, having been banished by the "Directory of Public Worship" since 1645. So late as July 1, 1660, Pepys records attending a service in the Abbey, and adds "No Common Prayer yet." If we find ourselves wondering why the Anglican party should have been so powerful in 1660, our wonder ought not to be greater than is excited by the power of the Puritan party when Laud was put to death. Both parties were, on each occasion, in a minority. Though England has never been long priest-ridden, it has often been priest-led.

The Convention Parliament did all that was expected of it. It was, however irregularly summoned, a truly representative assembly. Its members all swore—what will not members of Parliament swear?—that the king was supreme in Church and State, the only rightful king of the realm and of all other his dominions, and that from their hearts they abhorred, detested, and abjured the damnable doctrine that princes, excommunicated or deprived of the Pope, might be murdered by their subjects. They proceeded to pass a very useful Act of Indemnity and Oblivion, agreeing to let bygones be bygones, except in certain named cases. They ordered Mr. John Milton to be taken into custody, and prosecuted (which he never was) by the Attorney-General. Later on the poet was released from custody, and we find Mr. Marvell complaining to the House that their sergeant had extracted £150 in fees before he would let Mr. Milton go. On which Sir Heneage Finch, afterwards Lord Chancellor, laconically observed that Milton deserved hanging. He certainly got off easily, but, as he lived to publish *Paradise Lost*, *Paradise Regained*, and *Samson Agonistes*, he may be said to have earned his freedom. All his poetry put together never brought him in a third of the sum the sergeant got for letting him out of prison. General Monk, the man-midwife, who so skilfully assisted at that great Birth of Time, the Restoration, was made a duke, and Cromwell's army, so long the force behind the supreme power, was paid its arrears and (two regiments excepted) disbanded. "Fifty thousand men," says Macaulay, "accustomed to the profession of arms, were thrown upon the world ... in a few months there remained not a trace indicating that the most formidable army in the world had just been absorbed in the mass of the community."[1]

After this the House of Commons fell to discussing religion, and made the sad discovery that differences of opinion still existed. In these circumstances they decided to refer the matter to their pious king, and to such divines as he might choose. They then voted large sums of money for the royal establishment, and, it being the very end of August, adjourned till the 6th of November. As for making constitutional terms with the king, they never attempted it, though Sir Matthew Hale is credited with an attempt to induce them to do so. Any proposals of the kind must have failed. The people were in no mood for making constitutions.

Having met again on the 6th of November, Marvell, in a letter to the Mayor and Aldermen of Hull, dated the 27th of the month, reports that "the House fell upon the making out of the King's revenue to £1,200,000 a year." "The Customs are estimated toward £500,000 per annum in the revenue. His lands and fee farms £250,000. The Excise of Beer and Ale £300,000, the rest arise out of the Post Office, Wine Licenses, Stannaries Court, Probate of Wills, Post-fines, Forests, and other rights of the Crown. The excise of Foreign

Commodities is to be continued apart until satisfaction of public debts and engagements secured upon the excise."

This settlement of revenue marks "the beginning of a time." Cromwell, as Cowley puts it in his *Discourse*, by far the ablest indictment of Oliver ever penned, "took armes against two hundred thousand pounds a year, and raised them himself to above two millions." It is true. Cromwell spent the money honestly and efficiently, and chiefly on a navy that enabled him to wrest the command of the sea from the Dutch, to secure the carrying trade, and to challenge the world for supremacy in the Indies, both East and West. In doing this, he had the instinct of the whole nation behind him. But it was expensive.

Had Charles been the most honest and thrifty of men, instead of one of the most dishonest and extravagant, he must have found his financial position a very difficult one. He was poorer than Cromwell. The feudal taxation had fallen into desuetude. To revive wardships, etc., was impossible, to recover arrears hopeless. There was nothing for it but scientific taxation. One of his first Acts contains a schedule of taxed articles extending over fifteen double-columned pages of a quarto volume. To raise this revenue was difficult—in fact impossible, and the amount actually obtained was always far below the estimates.

Marvell's letter concludes thus:—

"To-morrow is the Bill for enacting his Majesty's declaration in religious matters and to have its first reading. It is said that on Sunday next Doctor Reynolds shall be created Bishop of Norwich."

The rumour about Reynolds's bishopric proved to be true. The new bishop was a very "moderate" Anglican indeed, and his appointment was meant as a sop to the Presbyterians. Richard Baxter and Edmund Calamy refused similar preferment.

On the 29th of November Marvell's letter contains the following passage:—

"Yesterday the Bill of the King's Declaration in religious matters was read for the first time; but upon the question for a second reading 'twas carried 183 against 157 in the negative, so there is an end of that Bill and for those excellent things therein. We must henceforth rely only upon his Majesty's goodness, who, I must needs say, hath hitherto been more ready to give than we to receive."

It is a noticeable feature of this correspondence that Marvell seldom mentions which way he voted himself.

The letter of the 4th of December contains some interesting matter:—

"GENTLEMEN,—Since my last, upon Thursday, the Bill for Vicarages hath been carryed up to the Lords; and a Message to them from our House that they would expedite the Bill for confirmation of Magna Charta, that for confirmation of marriages, and other bills of publick concernment, which haue laid by them euer since our last sitting, not returned to us. We had then the Bill for six moneths assesment in consideration, and read the Bill for taking away Court of Wards and Purveyance, and establishing the moiety of the Excise of Beere and ale in perpetuum, about which we sit euery afternoon in a Grand Committee. Upon Sunday last were consecrated in the Abby at Westminster, Doctor Cossins, Bishop of Durham, Sterne of Carlile, Gauden of Exeter, Ironside of Bristow, Loyd of Landaffe, Lucy of St. Dauids, Lany, the seuenth, whose diocese I remember not at present, and to-day they keep their feast in Haberdasher's hall, in London. Dr. Reinolds was not of the number, who is intended for Norwich. A Congedelire is gone down to Hereford for Dr. Monk, the Generall's brother, at present Provost of Eaton. 'Tis thought that since our throwing out the Bill of the King's Declaration, Mr. Calamy, and other moderate men, will be resolute in refusing of Bishopricks.... To-day our House was upon the Bill of Attainder of those that haue been executed, those that are fled, and of Cromwell, Bradshaw, Ireton, and Pride, and 'tis ordered that the carkasses and coffins of the four last named, shall be drawn with what expedition possible, upon an hurdle to Tyburn, there (to) be hanged up for a while, and then buryed under the gallows....

"WESTMINSTER, *Dec. 4, 1660.*"

Marvell's cool reporting of the hideous indignity inflicted upon his old master, and allowing it to pass *sub silentio*, is one of the many occasions that stirred Mr. Grosart's wonder. Nerves were tough in those days. Pepys tells us unconcernedly enough how, after seeing Lord Southampton sworn in at the Court of Exchequer as Lord Treasurer, he noticed "the heads of Cromwell, Bradshaw, and Ireton set up at the further end of Westminster Hall." It is quite possible Lady Fauconberg may have seen the same sight.[1]

The Convention Parliament was dissolved on the 29th of December 1660.

On 1st April 1661 Marvell was returned for the third and last time for Hull, for Charles the Second's first Parliament was of unconscionable long duration, not being dissolved till January 1679, after Marvell's death. It is known in history as the Pensionary or Long Parliament. The election figures were as below:—

| Colonel Gilbey, | 294 |
| Mr. Andrew Marvell, | 240 |

| Mr. Edward Barnard, | 195 |
| Mr. John Ramsden, | 122 |

Marvell was not present at or before the election, for on the 6th of April he writes:—

"I perceive by Mr. Mayor that you have again (as if it were grown a thing of course) made choice of me now, the third time, to serve for you in Parliament, which as I cannot attribute to anything but your constancy, so shall I, God willing, as in gratitude obliged, with no less constancy and vigour continue to execute your commands and study your service."

A word may here be said about payment of borough members. The members' fee was 6s. 8d. for every day the Parliament lasted. The wages were paid by the corporation out of the borough funds. It was never a popular charge. Burgesses in many places cared as little for M.P.'s as do some of their successors for free libraries. Prynne, perhaps the greatest parliamentary lawyer that ever lived, told Pepys one day, as they were driving to the Temple, that the number of burgesses to be returned to Parliament for any particular borough was not, for aught Prynne could find, fixed by law, but was at first left to the discretion of the sheriff, and that several boroughs had complained of the sheriff's putting them to the charge of sending up burgesses.

In August 1661 the corporation paid Marvell £28 for his fee as one of their burgesses, being 6s. 8d. a day for eighty-four days, the length of the Convention Parliament. Marvell continued to take his wages until the end of his days; but it is perhaps a mistake to suppose he was the very last member to do so. It was, however, unusual in Marvell's time.[1]

This Pensionary Parliament, though of a very decided "Church and King" complexion, was not in its original composition a body lacking character or independence, but it steadily deteriorated in both respects. Vacancies, as they occurred, and they occurred very frequently in those days of short lives, were filled up by courtiers and pensioners.

In the small tract, entitled *Flagellum Parliamentum*, which is a highly libellous "Dod," often attributed to Marvell, a record is preserved of more than two hundred members of this Parliament in 1675. Despite some humorous touches, this *Flagellum Parliamentum* is still disagreeable to read. But the most graphic picture we have of this Parliament is to be found in one of Lord Shaftesbury's political tracts entitled "A letter from a Parliament man to his Friend" (1675):—

"SIR,—I see you are greatly scandalized at our slow and confused Proceedings. I confess you have cause enough; but were you but within these walls for one half day, and saw the strange make and complexion that this house is of, you would wonder as much that ever you wondered at it; for we are such a pied Parliament, that none can say of what colour we are; for we consist of Old Cavaliers, Old Round-Heads, Indigent-Courtiers, and true Country Gentlemen: the two latter are most numerous, and would in probability bring things to some issue were they not clogged with the numerous uncertainties of the former. For the Old Cavalier, grown aged, and almost past his vice, is damnable godly and makes his doting piety more a plague to the world than his debauchery was, for he is so much a by-got to the B(ishop) that he forces his Loyalty to strike sail to his Religion, and could be content to pare the nails a little of the Civil Government, so you would but let him sharpen the Ecclesiastical Talons: which behaviour of his so exasperates the Round-Head, that he on the other hand cares not what increases the Interest of the Crown receives, so he can but diminish that of the miter: so that the Round-Head had rather enslave the Man than the Conscience: the Cavalier rather the Conscience than the Man; there being a sufficient stock of animosity as proper matter to work upon. Upon these, therefore, the Courtier mutually plays, for if any Ante-court motion be made he gains the Round-Head either to oppose or absent by telling them, If they will join him now he will join them for Liberty of Conscience. And when any affair is started on behalf of the Country he assures the Cavaliers, If they will then stand by him he will then join with them in promoting a Bill against the fanatics. Thus play they on both hands.... Wherefore it were happy that he had neither Round-Head nor Cavalier in the House, for they are each of them so prejudicate against the other that their sitting here signifies nothing but their fostering their old venom and lying at catch to stop every advantage to bear down each other, though it be in the destruction of their country. For if the Round-Heads bring in a good bill the Old Cavalier opposes it, for no other reason but because they brought it in."[1]

Such was the theatre of Marvell's public actions for the rest of his days, and if at times he may need forgiveness for the savagery of his satire, it ought to be found easy to forgive him.

The two members for Hull were soon immersed in matters of much local importance. They began by quarrelling with one another, Marvell writing "the bond of civility betwixt Col. Gilby and myself being unhappily snappt in pieces, and in such manner that I cannot see how it is possible ever to knit them again." House of Commons quarrels are usually soon made up, and so was this one. The custom was for *both* members to sign these letters, though they are all written in Marvell's hand—but if this was for any reason inconvenient, Marvell signed alone. No letters, unless in Marvell's writing, are preserved at Hull, which is a curious fact.

One of these bits of local business related to a patent alleged to have been granted by the Crown to certain persons, authorising them to erect and maintain *ballast wharfs* in the various ports, and to make charges in respect of them. This was resented by the members for the ports, and on Marvell's motion the matter was referred to the Committee of Grievances, before whom the patentees were summoned. When they came it appeared that the patent warranted none of the exactions that had been demanded, and also that the warrant sent down to Hull naming these charges was nothing more than a draft framed by the patentees themselves, and not authorised in any way. The patent was at once suspended. Marvell, like a true member of Parliament, wishes to get any little local credit that may be due for such prompt action, and writes:—

"In this thing (although I count all things I can do for your service to be mere trifles, and not worth taking notice of in respect of what I owe you) I must do myself that right to let you know that I, and I alone, have had the happiness to do that little which hitherto is effected."

The matter required delicate handling, for a reason Marvell gives: "Because, if the King's right in placing such impositions should be weakened, neither should he have power to make a grant of them to you."

Another much longer business related to a lighthouse, which some outsiders were anxious to build in the Humber. The corporation of Hull, acting on Marvell's advice, had petitioned the Privy Council, and were asked by their business-like member "to send us up a dormant credit for an hundred pound, which we yet indeed have no use of, but if need be must have ready at hand to reward such as will not otherwise befriend your business." Some months later Marvell forwards an account, not of the £100, but of the legal expenses about the lighthouse. He wishes it were less, but hopes that the "vigorous resistance" will discourage the designers from proceeding farther. This it did not do. As a member of the bar, I find two or three of the items in this old-world Bill of Costs interesting:—

To Mr. Scroggs to attend the Council,	£3 6 0
,, ,, ,, again for the same,	3 6 0
Spent on Mr. Scroggs at dinner,	18 0
To Mr. Scroggs again,	3 0 0
Fees of the Council Table,	1 10 0
Fee to Clerk of the Council,	2 0 0
For dinner for Mr. Scroggs and wine after,	1 0 0

To Mr. Cresset (the Solicitor),	20 0 0
To Mr. Scroggs for a dinner,	1 0 0

The barrister who was so frequently "refreshed" by Marvell lived to become "the infamous Lord Chief Justice Scroggs" of all school histories.

A week before the prorogation of Parliament, which happened on the 19th of May 1662, Marvell went to Holland and remained there for nine months, for he did not return until the very end of March 1663, more than a month after the reassembling of the House.

What took him there nobody knows. Writing to the Trinity House about the lighthouse business on the 8th of May 1662, Marvell says:—

"But that which troubles me is that by the interest of some persons too potent for me to refuse, and who have a great direction and influence upon my counsels and fortune, I am obliged to go beyond sea before I have perfected it (*i.e.* the lighthouse business). But first I do thereby make my Lord Carlisle (who is a member of the Privy Council and one of them to whom your business is referred) absolutely yours. And my journey is but into Holland, from whence I shall weekly correspond as if I were at London with all the rest of my friends, towards the affecting your business. Then I leave Col. Gilbey there, whose ability for business and affection to yours is such that I cannot be wanted though I am missing."

It is plain from this that Lord Carlisle is one of the powerful persons referred to—but beyond this we cannot go.

Whilst in Holland Marvell wrote both to the Trinity House and to the corporation on business matters.

In March 1663 Marvell came back in a hurry, some complaints having been made in Hull about his absence. He begins his first letter after his return as follows:—

"Being newly arrived in town and full of business, yet I could not neglect to give you notice that this day (2nd April 1663) I have been in the House and found my place empty, though it seems, as I now hear, that some persons would have been so courteous as to have filled it for me."

In none of these letters is any reference made to the debates in the House on the unhappy Bill of Uniformity, nor does any record of those discussions anywhere exist. The Savoy Conference proved a failure, and no lay reader of Baxter's account of it can profess wonder. Not a single point in difference was settled. In the meantime the restored Houses of Convocation, from which the Presbyterian members were excluded, had completed their revision of the Book of Common Prayer and presented it to Parliament.

In considering the Bill for Uniformity, the House of Lords, where Presbyterianism was powerfully represented, showed more regard for those "tender consciences" to which the king (by the new Prayer Book called for the first time "our most religious King") had referred in his Breda Declaration than did the House of Commons. "The Book, the whole Book, and nothing but the Book" was, in effect, the cry of the lower House, and on the 19th of May, ten days after Marvell had left for the Continent, the Act of Uniformity became law, and by the 24th of August 1662 all beneficed ministers and schoolmasters had to make the celebrated subscription and profession, or go out into the wilderness.

There has always been a dispute as to the physical possibility of perusing the compilation in question before the day fixed by the Statute. The Book was advertised for sale in London on the 6th of August, but how many copies were actually available on that day is not known.

The Dean and Chapter of Peterborough did not get their copies until the 17th of August. When the new folios reached the lonely parsonages of Cumberland and Durham—who would care to say? The Act required a verbal avowal of "unfeigned assent and consent to all and everything contained and prescribed in and by the Book of Common Prayer, and administrations of the Sacraments and other rites and ceremonies of the Church according to the use of the Church of England, together with the Psalter, and the form of manner of making, ordaining, and consecrating Bishops, Priests, and Deacons" to be made after the service upon "some Lord's day" before the Feast of St. Bartholomew, *i.e.* the 24th of August 1662. The Act also required subscription within the same time-limit to a declaration of (*inter alia*) uniformity to the Liturgy of the Church of England "as it is now by law established."

That this haste was indecent no layman is likely to dispute, but that it wrought practical wrong is doubtful. The Vicar of Bray needed no time to read his new Folio to enable him to make whatever avowal concerning it the law demanded; and as for signing the declaration, all he required for that purpose was pen and ink. Neither had the incumbent, who was a good churchman at heart, any doubts to settle. He rejoiced to know that his side was once more uppermost, and that it would be no longer necessary for him, in order to retain his living, to pretend to tolerate a Presbyterian, or to submit to read in his church the Directory of Public Worship. Convocation had approved the new Prayer Book, which was in substance the old one, and what more did any churchman require? As for the Presbyterians and others who were in possession of livings, the failure of the Savoy Conference must have made it plain to them that the Church of England had not allowed the king to keep his word, that compromise and comprehension had failed, and that if they were to remain where they were, it could only be on terms of completely severing themselves from all other Protestant bodies in the world, and becoming thorough Episcopalians. No Presbyterian of any eminence was prepared to make the statutory avowal. Painful as it always must be to give up any good thing by a fixed date, it is hard to see what advantage would have accrued from delay.

When the day came, some two thousand parsons were turned out of the Church of England. Among them were included many of the most devout and some of the most learned of our divines. Their "coming in" had been irregular, their "going out" was painful.

Save so far as it turned these men out, the Act was a failure. It did not procure that uniformity in the public worship of God which it declared was so desirable; it prevented no scandal; it arrested no decay; it allayed no distemper, and it certainly did not settle the peace of the Church. Inside the Church the bishops were supine, the parochial clergy indifferent, and the worshippers, if such a name can properly be bestowed upon the congregations, were grossly irreverent. Nor was any improvement in the conduct of the Church service noticeable until after the Revolution, and when legislation had conceded a somewhat shabby measure of toleration to those who by that time had become rigid, traditional, and hereditary dissenters. Then indeed some attempts began to be made to secure a real uniformity of ritual in the public worship of the Church of England.[1] How far success has rewarded these exertions it is not for me to say.

Marvell did not remain long at home after his return from Holland. A strange adventure lay before him. He thus introduces it in a letter dated 20th June 1663:—

"GENTLEMEN, MY VERY WORTHY FRIENDS,—The relation I have to your affairs, and the intimacy of that affection I ow you, do both incline and oblige me to communicate to you, that there is a probability I may very shortly have occasion to go beyond sea; for my Lord of Carlisle being chosen by his Majesty, Embassadour Extraordinary to Muscovy, Sweden, and Denmarke, hath used his power, which ought to be very great with me, to make me goe along with him Secretary in those embassages. It is no new thing for Members of our House to be dispens'd with for the service of the King and Nation in forain parts. And you may be sure that I will not stirre without speciall leave of the House; that so you may be freed from any possibility of being importuned or tempted to make any other choice, in my absence. However, I can not but advise also with you, desiring to take your assent along with me, so much esteeme I have both of your prudence and friendship. The time allotted for the embassy is not much above a yeare: probably it may not be much less betwixt our adjournment and next meeting; and, however, you have Colonell Gilby, to whom my presence can make little addition, so that if I cannot decline this voyage, I shall have the comfort to believe, that, all things considered, you cannot thereby receive any disservice. I shall hope to receive herein your speedy answer...."

What was the "power" Lord Carlisle had over Marvell is not now discoverable, but the tie, whatever it may have been, was evidently a close one.

A month after this letter Marvell started on his way.

"GENTLEMEN, MY VERY WORTHY FRIENDS,—Being this day taking barge for Gravesend, there to embark for Archangel, so to Muscow, thence for Sweden, and last of all Denmarke; all of which I hope, by God's blessing, to finish within twelve moneths time: I do hereby, with my last and seriousest thoughts, salute you, rendring you all hearty thanks for your great kindnesse and friendship to me upon all occasions, and ardently beseeching God to keep you all in His gracious protection, to your own honour, and the welfare and flourishing of your Corporation, to which I am and shall ever continue a most affectionate and devoted servant. I undertake this voyage with the order and good liking of his Majesty, and by leave given me from the House and enterd in the Journal; and having received moreover your approbation, I go therefore with more ease and satisfaction of mind, and augurate to myselfe the happier successe in all my proceedings...."

It was Marvell's good fortune to be in Lord Carlisle's frigate which made the voyage to Archangel in less than a month, sailing from Gravesend on the 22nd of July and arriving at the bar of Archangel on the 19th of August. The companion frigate took seven weeks to compass the same distance.

Nothing of any importance attaches to this Russian embassy. It cost a great deal of money, took up a great deal of time, exposed the ambassador and his suite to much rudeness and discomfort, and failed to effect its main object, which was to secure a renewal of the privileges formerly enjoyed in Muscovy by British merchants.

One of the attendants upon the ambassador made a small book out of his travels, which did not get printed till 1669, when it attracted little notice. Mr. Grosart was the first of Marvell's many biographers to discover the existence of this narrative.[1] He found it in the first instance, to use his own language, "in one of good trusty John Harris' folios of *Travels and Voyages*" (two vols. folio, 1705); but later on he made the sad discovery that this "good trusty John Harris" had uplifted what he called his "true and particular account" from the book of 1669 without any acknowledgment. "For ways that are dark" the old compiler of travels was not easily excelled, but why should Mr. Grosart have gone out of his way to call an eighteenth-century book-maker, about whom he evidently knew nothing, "good and trusty"? Harris was never either the one or the other, and died a pauper!

A journey to Moscow in 1663-64 was no joke. Lord Carlisle, who was accompanied by his wife and eldest son, although ready to start from Archangel by the end of September, was doomed to spend both the 5th of November and Christmas Day in the gloomy town of Vologda, which they had reached, travelling by water, on the 17th of October. Some of this time was spent in quarrelling as to who was to supply the sledges that were required to convey the ambassador and all his *impedimenta* along the now ice-bound roads to Moscow. It was one of Marvell's many duties to remonstrate with the authorities for their cruel and disrespectful indifference; he did so with great freedom, but with no effect, and at last the ambassador was obliged to hire two hundred sledges at his own charges. Sixty he sent on ahead, following with one hundred and forty on the 15th of January 1664. It was an intensely cold journey, and the accommodation at night, with one happy exception, proved quite infamous. On the 3rd of February Lord Carlisle and his *cortége* found themselves five versts from Moscow. The 5th of February was fixed for their entry into the city in all their finery. They were ready on the morning of that day, awaiting the arrival of the Tsar's escort, but it never came. Lord Carlisle had sent his cooks on to Moscow to prepare the dinner he expected to eat in his city-quarters. Nightfall approached, and it was not till "half an hour before night" that the belated messengers arrived, full of excuses. The ambassador was hungry, cold, and furious, nor did his anger abate when told he was not to be allowed to enter Moscow that night, as the Tsar and his ladies were very anxious to enjoy the spectacle. The return of the cooks from Moscow and the preparation of dinner, though a mitigation, was no cure for wounded pride, and Lord Carlisle, calling Marvell to his side, and with his assistance, concocted a letter in Latin to the Tsar, complaining bitterly of their ill-treatment *inter fumosi gurgustii sordes et angustias sine cibo aut potu*, and going so far as to assert that had anything of the kind happened in England to a foreign ambassador, the King of England would never have rested until the offence had been atoned for with the blood of the criminals. When, some forty years afterwards, Peter the Great asked Queen Anne to chop off the heads of the rude men who had arrested his ambassador for debt, he had, perhaps, Marvell's letter before him.

On the 6th of February Lord Carlisle and his suite made their public entry into Moscow; but so long a time was occupied over the few versts they had to travel, that it was dusk before the Kremlin was reached.

The formal reception of the ambassador was on the 11th of February. Marvell was in the ambassador's sledge and carried his credentials upon a yard of red damask. The titles of the Russian Potentate would, if printed here, fill half a page. All the Russias, Great, Little, and White, emperies more than one, dukedoms by the dozen, territories, countries, and dominions—not all easy to identify on the map, and very hard to pronounce—were read out in a loud voice by Marvell. At the end of them came the homely title of the Earl and his offices, "his Majesty's Lieutenant in the Counties of Cumberland and Westmorland."

The letters read and delivered, the Tsar and his Boyars rose in their places simultaneously, and their tissue vests made so strange, loud, and unexpected a noise as to provoke the ever too easily moved risibility of the Englishmen.[1] When Marvell and the rest of them had ceased from giggling, the Tsar inquired after the health of the king, but the distance between his Imperial Majesty and Lord Carlisle being too great for the question to carry, it had to be repeated by those who were nearer the ambassador, who gravely replied that when he last saw his master, namely on the 20th of July then last past, he was perfectly well. To the same question as to the health of "the desolate widow of Charles the First," Carlisle returned the same cautious answer. He then read a very long speech in English, which his interpreter turned into Russian. The same oration was rendered into Latin by Marvell, and presented. Over Marvell's Latin trouble arose, for the Russians were bent on taking and giving offence. Marvell had styled the Tsar *Illustrissimus* when he ought, so it was alleged, to have called him *Serenissimus*. Marvell was not a schoolmaster's son, an old scholar of Trinity, and Milton's assistant as Latin Secretary for nothing. He prepared a reply which, as it does not lack humour, has a distinct literary flavour, and is all that came of the embassy, may here be given at length:—

"I reply, saith he, that I sent no such paper into the Embassy-office, but upon the desire of his Tzarskoy Majesty's Councellor Evan Offonassy Pronchissof, I delivered it to him, not being a paper of State, nor written in the English Language wherein I treat, nor put into the hands of the near Boyars and Councellors of his Tzarskoy majesty, nor subscribed by my self, nor translated into Russe by my Interpreter, but only as a piece of curiosity, which is now restored me, and I am possessed of it; so that herein his Tzarskoy majestie's near Boyars and Councellors are doubtless ill grounded. But again I say concerning the value of the words *Illustrissimus* and *Serenissimus* compared together, seeing we must here from affaires of State, fall into Grammatical contests concerning the Latin tongue; that the word *Serenus* signifieth nothing but still and calm; and, therefore, though of late times adopted into the Titles of great Princes by reason of that benigne tranquility which properly dwells in the majestick countenance of great Princes, and that venerable stillness of all the Attendants that surround them, of which I have seen an excellent example when I was in the presence of his Tzarskoy majesty, yet is more properly used concerning the calmness of the weather, or season. So that even the night is elegantly called *Serena* by the best Authors,

Cicero in Arato 12, Lucretius i. l. 29. '*Serena nox*'; and upon perusing again what I have writ in this paper, I finde that I have out of the customariness of that expression my self near the beginning said, And that most serene night, &c. Whereas on the contrary *Illustris* in its proper derivation and signification expresseth that which is all resplendent, lightsome, and glorious, as well without as within, and that not with a secondary but with a primitive and original light. For if the Sun be, as he is, the first fountain of light, and Poets in their expressions (as is well known) are higher by much than those that write in Prose, what else is it when Ovid in the 2. of the Metamorphoses saith of Phœbus speaking with Phaëthon, *Qui terque quaterque concutiens Illustre caput*, and the Latin Orators, as Pliny, Ep. 139, when they would say the highest thing that can be exprest upon any subject, word it thus, *Nihil Illustrius dicere possum*. So that hereby may appear to his Tzarskoy Majestie's near Boyars and Counsellors what diminution there is to his Tzarskoy Majesty (which farr be it from my thoughts) if I appropriate *Serenissimus* to my Master and *Illustrissimus* to Him than which *nihil dici potest Illustrius*. But because this was in the time of the purity of the Latin tongue, when the word *Serenus* was never used in the Title of any Prince or Person, I shall go on to deale with the utmost candor, forasmuch as in this Nation the nicety of that most eloquent language is not so perfectly understood, which gives occasion to these mistakes. I confess therefore that indeed in the declination of the Latin tongue, and when there scarce could be found out words enough to supply the modern ambition of Titles, Serenissimus as several other words hath grown in fashion for a compellation of lesser as well as greater Princes, and yet befits both the one and the other. So there is *Serenissima Respublica Veneta, Serenitates Electoriæ, Serenitates Regiæ,* even as the word Highness or *Celsitudo* befits a Duke, a Prince, a King, or an Emperour, adjoyning to it the respective quality, and so the word *Illustris*. But suppose it were by modern use (which I deny) depressed from the undoubted superiority that it had of *Serenus* in the purest antiquity, yet being added in the transcendent degree to the word Emperour, the highest denomination that a Prince is capable of, it becomes of the same value. So that to interpret *Illustrissimus* unto diminution is to find a positive in a superlative, and in the most orient light to seek for darkness. And I would, seeing the near Boyars and Counsellors of his Tzarskoy Majesty are pleased to mention the Title given to his Tzarskoy Majesty by his Cesarian Majesty, gladly be satisfied by them, whether ever any Cesarian Majesty writ formerly hither in High-Dutch, and whether then they styled his Tzarskoy Majesty Durchluchtigste which is the same with *Illustrissimus*, and which I believe the Cæsar hath kept for Himself. But to cut short, his Royal Majesty hath used the word to his Tzarskoy Majesty in his Letter, not out of imitation of others, although even in the Dutch Letter to his Tzarskoy Majesty of 16 June 1663, I finde Durchlauchtigste the same (as I said) with *Illustrissimus*, but out of the constant use of his own Court, further joyning before it Most High, Most Potent, and adding after it Great Lord Emperour, which is an higher Title than any Prince in the World gives his Tzarskoy Majesty, and as high a Title of honour as can be given to any thing under the Divinity. For the King my Master who possesses as considerable Dominions, and by as high and self-dependent a right as any Prince in the Universe, yet contenting Himself with the easiest Titles, and satisfying Himself in the essence of things, doth most willingly give to other Princes the Titles which are appropriated to them, but to the Tzarskoy Majesties of Russia his Royal Ancestors, and to his present Tzarskoy Majesty his Royal Majesty himself, have usually and do gladly pay Titles even to superfluity out of meer kindness. And upon that reason He added the word most Illustrious, and so did I use it in the Latin of my speech. Yet, that You may find I did not out of any criticisme of honor, but for distinction sake use it as I did, You may see in one place of the same speech *Serenitas*, speaking of his Tzarskoy Majesty: and I would have used *Serenissimus* an hundred times concerning his Tzarskoy Majesty, had I thought it would have pleased Him better. And I dare promise You that his Majesty will upon the first information from me stile him *Serenissimus*, and I (notwithstanding what I have said) shall make little difficulty of altering the word in that speech, and of delivering it so to You, with that protestation that I have not in using that word *Illustrissimus* erred nor used any diminution (which God forbid) to his Tzarskoy Majesty, but on the contrary after the example of the King my Master intended and shewed him all possible honor. And so God grant all happiness to His most high, most Potent, most Illustrious, and most Serene Tzarskoy Majesty, and that the friendship may daily increase betwixt His said Majesty and his most Serene Majesty my Master."

On the 19th of February the Tsar invited Lord Carlisle and his suite to a dinner, which, beginning at two o'clock, lasted till eleven, when it was prematurely broken up by the Tsar's nose beginning to bleed. Five hundred dishes were served, but there were no napkins, and the table-cloths only just covered the boards. There were Spanish wines, white and red mead, Puaz and strong waters. The English ambassador was not properly placed at table, not being anywhere near the Tsar, and his faithful suite shared his resentment. Time went on, but no diplomatic progress was made. The Tsar would not renew the privileges of the British merchants; Easter was spent in Moscow, May also—and still nothing was done. Carlisle, in a huff, determined to go away, and, somewhat to the distress of his followers, refused to accept the costly sables sent by the Tzar, not only to the ambassador, Lady Carlisle, and Lord Morpeth, but to the secretaries and others. The Tzar thereupon returned the plate which our king had sent him, which plate Lord Carlisle seems to have appropriated, no doubt with diplomatic correctness, as his perquisite in lieu of the sables; but the suite got nothing.

The embassy left Moscow on the 24th of June for Novgorod and Riga, and after visiting Stockholm and Copenhagen, Lord Carlisle and Marvell reached London on the 30th of January 1665.

During Marvell's absence war had been declared with the Dutch. It was never difficult to go to war with the Dutch. The king was always in want of money, and as no proper check existed over war supplies, he took what he wanted out of them. The merchants on 'Change desired war, saying that the trade of the world was too little for both England and Holland, and that one or the other "must down." The English manufacturers, who felt the sting of their Dutch competitors, were always in favour of war. Then the growing insolence of the Dutch in the Indies was not to be borne. Stories were circulated how the Hollanders had proclaimed themselves "Lords of the Southern Seas," and meant to deny English ships the right of entry in that quarter of the globe. A baronet called on Pepys and pulled out of his pocket letters from the East Indies, full of sad tales of Englishmen having been actually thrashed inside their own factory at Surat by swaggering Dutchmen, who had insulted the flag of St. George, and swore they were going to be the masters "out there." Pepys, who knew a little about the state of the royal navy, listened sorrowfully and was content to hope that the war would not come until "we are more ready for it."

In the House of Commons the prudent men were against the war, and were at once accused of being in the pay of the Dutch. The king's friends were all for the war, and nobody doubted that some of the money voted for it would find its way into their pockets, or at all events that pensions would reward their fidelity. A third group who favoured the war were supposed to do so because their disloyalty and fanaticism always disposed them to trouble the waters in which they wished to fish.

The war began in November 1664, and on the 24th of that month the king opened Parliament and demanded money. He got it. Clarendon describes how Sir Robert Paston from Norfolk, a back-bench man, "who was no frequent speaker, but delivered what he had a mind to say very clearly," stood up and proposed a grant of two and a half million pounds, to be spread over three years. So huge a sum took the House by surprise. Nobody spoke; "they sat in amazement." Somebody at last found his voice and moved a much smaller sum, but no one seconded him. Sir Robert Paston ultimately found supporters, "no man who had any relation to the Court speaking a word." The Speaker put Sir Robert Paston's motion as the question, "and the affirmative made a good sound, and very few gave their negative aloud." But Clarendon adds, "it was notorious very many sat silent."

The war was not in its early stages unpopular, being for the control of the sea, for the right of search, for the fishing trade, for mastery of the "gorgeous

East." The Admiralty had been busy, and a hundred frigates, well gunned, were ready for the blue water by February 1665. The Duke of York, who took the command, was a keen sailor, though his unhappy notions as to patronage, and its exercise, were fatal to an efficient service. On the 3rd of June the duke had his one victory; it was off the roadstead of Harwich, and the roar of his artillery was heard in Westminster. It was a fierce fight; the king's great friend, Charles Berkeley, just made a peer and about to be made a duke, Lord Muskerry and young Richard Boyle, all on the duke's ship the *Royal Charles*, were killed by one shot, their blood and brains flying in the duke's face. The Earls of Marlborough and Portland were killed. The gallant Lawson, who rose from the ranks in Cromwell's time, an Anabaptist and a Republican, but still in high command, received on board his ship, the *Royal Oak*, a fatal wound. On the other side the Dutch admiral, Opdam, was blown into the air with his ship and crew. The Dutch fleet was scattered, and fled, after a loss estimated at twenty-four ships and eight thousand men killed and wounded; England lost no ship and but six hundred men.

The victory was not followed up. Some say the duke lost nerve. Tromp was allowed to lead a great part of the fleet away in safety, and when the great De Ruyter was recalled from the West Indies he was soon able to assume the command of a formidable number of fighting craft.

In less than ten days after this great engagement the plague appeared in London, a terrible and a solemnising affliction, lasting the rest of the year. It was at its worst in September, when in one week more than seven thousand died of it. The total number of its dead is estimated at sixty-eight thousand five hundred and ninety-six.

On account of the plague Parliament was summoned to meet at Oxford in October 1665.

Marvell must have reached Oxford in good time, for the Admission Book of the Bodleian records his visit to the library on the last day of September. His first letter from Oxford is dated 15th October, and in it he tells the corporation that the House, "upon His Majesty's representation of the necessity of further supplies in reference to the Dutch War and probability of the French embracing their interests, hath voted the King £1,250,000 additional to be levied in two years." The king, who was the frankest of mortals in speech, though false as Belial in action, told the House that he had already spent all the money previously voted and must have more, especially if France was to prefer the friendship of Holland to his. Amidst loud acclamations the money was voted. The French ambassadors, who were in Oxford, saw for themselves the temper of Parliament.

Notwithstanding the terrible plight of the capital, Oxford was gaiety itself. The king was accompanied by his consort, who then was hopeful of an heir, and also by Lady Castlemaine and Miss Stewart. Lady Castlemaine did not escape the shaft of University wit, for a stinging couplet was set up during the night on her door, for the discovery of the authorship of which a reward of £1000 was offered. It may very well have been Marvell's.[1]

The Duke of Monmouth gave a ball to the queen and her ladies, where, after the queen's retirement, "Mrs. Stewart was extraordinary merry," and sang "French songs with great skill."[2]

Ten Acts of Parliament received the royal assent at Oxford, of which but one is still remembered in certain quarters—the Five Mile Act, which Marvell briefly describes as an Act "for debarring ejected Nonconformists from living in or near Corporations (where they had formerly pursued their callings), unless taking the new Oath and Declaration." Parliament was prorogued at the end of October.

Another visitation of Providence was soon to befall the capital. On Sunday morning, the 2nd of September, Pepys was aroused by one of his maid-servants at 3 A.M. to look at a fire. He could not make out much about it and went to bed again, but when he rose at seven o'clock it was still burning, so he left his house and made his way to the Tower, from whence he saw London Bridge aflame, and describes how the poor pigeons, loth to leave their homes, fluttered about the balconies, until with singed wings they fell into the flames. After gazing his fill he went to Whitehall and had an interview with the king, who at once ordered his barge and proceeded downstream to his burning City, and to the assistance of a distracted Lord Mayor.

The fire raged four days, and made an end of old London, a picturesque and even beautiful City. St. Paul's, both the church and the school, the Royal Exchange, Ludgate, Fleet Street as far as the Inner Temple, were by the 7th of the month smoking ruins. Four hundred streets, eighty-nine churches (just a church an hour, so the curious noted), warehouses unnumbered with all their varied contents, whole editions of books, valuable and the reverse of valuable, were wiped out of existence. Rents to an enormous amount ceased to be represented any longer by the houses that paid them. How was the king to get his chimney-money? How were merchants to meet their obligations? The parsons on Sunday, the 9th of September, ought to have had no difficulty in finding texts for their sermons. Pepys went to church twice, but without edification, and certainly Dean Harding, whom he heard complaining in the evening "that the City had been reduced from a folio to a duo decimo," hardly rose to the dignity of the occasion.

Strange to say, not a life was actually lost in the fire,[1] though some old Londoners (among them Edmund Calamy's grandfather) died of grief, and others (and among them Shirley the dramatist and his wife) from exposure and exhaustion. One hysterical foreigner, who insisted that he lit the flame, was executed, though no sensible man believed what he said. It was long the boast of the merchants of London that no one of their number "broke" in consequence of the great fire.

Unhappily the belief was widespread, as that "tall bully," the monument, long testified, that the fire was the work of the Roman Catholics, and aliens, suspected of belonging to our old religion, found it dangerous to walk the streets whilst the embers still smoked, which they continued to do for six months.

The meeting of Parliament was a little delayed in consequence of this national disaster, and when it did meet at the end of the month, Marvell reports the appointment of two Committees, one "about the Fire of London," and the other "to receive informations of the insolence of the Popish priests and Jesuits, and of the increase of Popery." The latter Committee almost at once reported to the House, to quote from Marvell's letter of the 27th of October, "that his Majesty be desired to issue out his proclamation that all Popish priests and Jesuits, except such as not being natural-born subjects, or belong to the Queen Mother and Queen Consort, be banished in thirty days or else the law be executed upon them, that all Justices of Peace and officers concerned put the laws in execution against Papists and suspected Papists in order to their execution, and that all officers, civil or military, not taking the Oaths of Supremacy and Allegiance within twenty days be displaced."

In a very real sense the great fire of London continued to smoke for many a weary year, and to fill the air with black suspicions and civil discord.

Parliament had not sat long before it was discovered that a change had taken place in its temper and spirit. The plague and the fire had contributed to this change. The London clergy had not exhibited great devotion during the former affliction. Many of the incumbents deserted their flocks, and their empty pulpits had been filled by zealots, who preached "Woe unto Jerusalem." The profligacy of the Court, and the general decay of manners, when added to the severity of the legislation against the Nonconformists, gave the ejected clergy opportunities for a renewal of their spiritual ministrations, and as usual their labours, *pro salute animarum*, aroused political dissatisfaction. Some of the more outrageous supporters of the royal prerogative, the renegade May among them, professed to see in the fire a punishment upon the spirit of freedom, for which the City had once been famous, and urged the king not to suffer it to be rebuilt again "to be a bit in his mouth and a bridle upon his neck, but to keep it all open," and that his troops might enter whenever he thought necessary, "there being no other way to govern that rude multitude but by force."

Rabid nonsense of this kind had no weight with the king, who never showed his native good sense more conspicuously than in the pains he took over the rebuilding of London; but none the less it had its effect in getting rid once and for ever of that spirit of excessive (besotted is Hallam's word) loyalty which had characterised the Restoration.

The king, of course, wanted money, nor was Parliament disposed to refuse it, we being still at war with Holland; but to the horror of that elderly pedant, Lord Clarendon, the Commons passed a Bill appointing a commission of members of both Houses "to inspect"—I am now quoting Marvell—"and examine thoroughly the former expense of the £2,800,000, of the £1,250,000 of the Militia money, of the prize goods, etc." In an earlier letter Marvell attributes the new temper of Parliament, "not to any want of ardour to supply the public necessities, but out of our House's sense also of the burden to be laid upon the subject." Clarendon was so alarmed that he advised a dissolution. Charles was alarmed, too, knowing well that both Carteret, the Treasurer of the Navy, and Lord Ashley, the Treasurer of the Prize Money, issued out many sums upon the king's warrant, for which no accounts could be produced, but he was still more frightened of a new Parliament. In the present Parliament he had, so Clarendon admits, "a hundred members of his own menial servants and their near relations." The bishops were also against a dissolution, dreading the return of Presbyterian members, so Clarendon's advice was not followed, and the king very reluctantly consented to the commission, about which Pepys has so much to say. It did not get appointed at once, but when it did Pepys rejoices greatly that its secretary, Mr. Jessopp, was "an old fashioned Cromwell man"; in other words, both honest and efficient.

The shrewd Secretary of the Navy Office here puts his finger on the real plague-spot of the Restoration. Our Puritan historians write rather loosely about "the floodgates of dissipation," etc., having been flung open by that event as if it had wrought a sudden change in human nature. Mr. Pepys, whose frank Diary begins during the Protectorate, underwent no such change. He was just the same sinner under Cromwell as he was under Charles. Sober, grave divines may be found deploring the growing profligacy of the times long before the 29th of May 1660. An era of extravagance was evidently to be expected. No doubt the king's return assisted it. No country could be anything but the worse for having Charles the Second as its "most religious King." The Restoration of the Stuarts was the best "excuse for a glass" ever offered to an Englishman. He availed himself of it with even more than his accustomed freedom. But it cannot be said that the king's debauchery was ever approved of even in London. Both the mercurial Pepys and the grave Evelyn alike deplore it. The misfortune clearly attributable to the king's return was the substitution of a corrupt, inefficient, and unpatriotic administration for the old-fashioned servants of the public whom Cromwell had gathered round him.

Parliament was busy with new taxes. In November 1666 Marvell writes:—

"The Committee has prepared these votes. All persons shall pay one shilling per poll, all aliens two, all Nonconformists and papists two, all servants one shilling in the pound of their wages, all personal estates shall pay for so much as is not already taxed by the land-tax, after twenty shillings in the hundred. Cattle, corn, and household furniture shall be excepted, and all such stock-in-trade as is already taxed by the land-tax, but the rest to be liable."

Stringent work! Later on we read:—

"Three shillings in the pound for all offices and public employments, except military; lawyers and physicians proportionate to their practice."

Here is the income-tax long before Mr. Pitt.

The House of Lords, trembling on the verge of a breach of privilege, altered this Poll Bill. Marvell writes in January 1667:—

"We have not advanced much this week; the alterations of the Lords upon the Poll Bill have kept us busy. We have disagreed in most. Aliens we adhere to pay double. Nonconformists we agree with them *not* to pay double (126 to 91), to allow no exemptions from patents to free from paying, we adhere; and we also rejected a long clause whereby they as well as the Commoners pretend distinctly to give to the King, and to-day we send up our reasons."

The Lords agreed, and the Bill passed.

Ireland supplied a very stormy measure. I am afraid Marvell was on the wrong side, but owing to his reserve I am not sure. An Irish Cattle Bill was a measure very popular in the House of Commons, its object being to prevent Ireland from sending over live beasts to be fattened, killed, and consumed in England. You can read all about it in Clarendon's *Life* (vol. iii. pp. 704-720, 739), and think you are reading about Canadian cattle to-day. The breeders (in a majority) were on one side, and the owners of pasture-land on the other. The breeders said the Irish cattle were bred in Ireland for nothing and transported for little, that they undersold the English-bred cattle, and consequently "the breed of Cattle in the Kingdom was totally given over," and rents fell. Other members contended in their places "that their countries had no land bad enough to breed, and that their traffic consisted in buying lean cattle and making them fat, and upon this they paid their rent." Nobody, except the king, gave a thought to Ireland. He, in this not unworthy of his great Tudor predecessor, Henry the Eighth, declared he was King of Ireland no less than of England, and would do nothing to injure one portion of his dominions for the benefit of another. But as usual he gave way, being in great straits for money. The House of Lords was better disposed towards Ireland than the House of Commons, but they too yielded to selfish clamour, and the Bill, which had excited great fury, became law, and proved ineffective, owing (as was alleged) to that corruption which restrictions on trade seem to have the trick of breeding.[1]

It is always agreeable to be reminded that however large a part of our history is composed of the record of passion, greed, delusion, and stupidity, yet common-sense, the love of order and of justice (in matters of business), have usually been the predominant factors in our national life, despite priest, merchant, and party.

Nowhere is this better illustrated than by two measures to which Marvell refers as Bills "for the prevention of lawsuits between landlord and tenant" and for "the Rebuilding of London." Both these Bills became law in February 1668, within five months of the great catastrophe that was their occasion. Two more sensible, well-planned, well-drawn, courageous measures were never piloted through both Houses. King, Lords and Commons, all put their heads together to face a great emergency and to provide an immediate remedy.

The Bill to prevent lawsuits is best appreciated if we read its preamble:—

"Whereas the greatest part of the houses in the City of London having been burnt by the dreadful and dismal fire which happened in September last, many of the Tenants, under-tenants, and late occupiers are liable unto suits and actions to compel them to repair and to rebuild the same, and to pay their rents as if the same had not been burnt, and are not relievable therefor in any ordinary course of law; and great differences are likely to arise concerning the Repairs and rebuilding the said houses, and payment of rents which, if they should not be determined with speed and without charge, would much obstruct the rebuilding of the s^d City. And for that it is just that everyone concerned should bear a proportionate share of this loss according to their several interests wherein in respect of the multitude of cases, varying in their circumstances, no certain general rule can be prescribed."

After this recital it was enacted that the judges of the King's Bench and Common Pleas and the Barons of the Exchequer, or any three or more of them, should form a Court of Record to hear and determine every possible dispute or difference arising out of the great fire, whether relating to liability to repair, and rebuild, or to pay rent, or for arrears of rent (other than arrears which had accrued due before the 1st of September) or otherwise howsoever. The proceedings were to be by summary process, *sine forma et figura judicii* and without court fees. The judges were to be bound by no rules either of law or equity, and might call for what evidence they chose, including that of the interested parties, and try the case as it best could be tried. Their orders were to be final and not (save in a single excepted case) subject to any appeal. All persons in remainder and reversion were to be bound by these orders, although infants, married women, idiots, beyond seas, or under any other disability. A special power was given to order the surrender of existing leases, and to grant new ones for terms not exceeding forty years. The judges gave their services for nothing, and, for once, released from all their own trammels, set to work to do substantial justice between landlord and tenant, personalty and realty, the life interest and the remainder, covenantor and covenantee, after a fashion which excited the admiration and won the confidence of the whole City. The ordinary suitor, still left exposed to the pitfalls of the special pleader, the risks (owing to the exclusion of evidence) of a non-suit and the costly cumbersomeness of the Court of Chancery, must often have wished that the subject-matter of his litigation had perished in the flames of the great fire.

This court sat in Clifford's Inn, and was usually presided over by Sir Matthew Hale, whose skill both as an arithmetician and an architect completed his fitness for so responsible a position. Within a year the work was done.

The Act for rebuilding the City is an elaborate measure of more than forty clauses, and aimed at securing "the regularity, safety, conveniency and beauty" of the new London that was to be. The buildings were classified according to their position and character, and had to maintain a prescribed level of quality. The materials to be employed were named. New streets were to be of certain widths, and so on. This is the Act that contains the first Betterment Clause: "And forasmuch as the Houses now remaining and to be rebuilt will receive more or less advantage in the value of the rents by the liberty of air and free recourse for trade," it was enacted that a jury might be sworn to assess upon the owners and others interested of and in the said houses, such sum or sums of money with respect of their several interests "in consideration of such improvement and melioration as in reason and good conscience they shall think fit."

It takes nothing short of a catastrophe to suspend in England, even for a few months, those rules of evidence that often make justice impossible, and those rights of landlords which for centuries have appropriated public expenditure to private gain.[1]

The moneys required to pay for the land taken under the Act to widen streets and to accomplish the other authorised works were raised, as Marvell informs his constituents, by a tax of twelve pence on every chaldron of coal coming as far as Gravesend. Few taxes have had so useful and so harmless a life.

All this time the Dutch War was going on, but the heart was out of it. Nothing in England is so popular as war, except the peace that comes after it. The king now wanted peace, and the merchants on 'Change had glutted their ire. In February 1667 the king told the Houses of Parliament that all "sober" men would be glad to see peace. Unluckily, it seems to have been assumed that we could have peace whenever we wanted it, and the fatal error was committed of at once "laying up" the first-and second-rate ships. It thus came about that, whilst still at war, England had no fleet to put to sea. It did not at first seem likely that the overtures for peace would present much difficulty, when suddenly arose the question of Poleroone. It is amazing how few Englishmen have ever heard of Poleroone, or even of the Banda Islands, of which group it is one. Indeed, a more insignificant speck in the ocean it would be hard to find. To discover it on an atlas is no easy task. Yet, but for Poleroone, the Dutch would never have taken Sheerness, or broken the chain at Gillingham, or carried away with them to the Texel the proud vessel that had brought back Charles the Second to an excited population.

Poleroone is a small nutmeg-growing island in the Indian Archipelago, not far from the eastern extremity of New Guinea. King James the First imagined he had some right to it, and, at any rate, Oliver Cromwell, when he made peace with the Dutch, made a great point of Poleroone. Have it he would for the East India Company. The Dutch objected, but gave way, and by an article in the treaty with Oliver bound themselves to give up Poleroone to the Company. All, in fact, that they did do, was to cut down the nutmeg trees, and so make the island good for nothing for many a long year. Physical possession was never taken. For some unaccountable reason Charles, who had sold Oliver's Dunkirk to the French for half a million of money, stuck out for Poleroone. What Cromwell had taken he was not going to give up! On the other hand, neither would the Dutch give up Poleroone. This dispute, about a barren island, delayed the settlement of the peace preliminaries; but eventually the British plenipotentiaries did get out to Breda, in May 1667. Our sanguine king expected an immediate cessation of hostilities, and that his unpreparedness would thus be huddled up. All of a sudden, at the beginning of June, De Ruyter led out his fleet, and with a fair wind behind him stood for the Thames. All is fair in war. England was caught napping. The doleful history reads like that of a sudden piratical onslaught, and reveals the fatal inefficiency of the administration. Sheerness was practically defenceless. "There were a Company or two of very good soldiers there under excellent officers, but the fortifications were so weak and unfinished, and all other provisions so entirely wanting, that the Dutch Fleet no sooner approached within a distance but with their cannon they beat all the works flat and drove all the men from the ground, which, as soon as they had done with their Boats, they landed men and seemed resolved to fortify and keep it."[1] Capture of Sheerness by the Dutch! No need of a halfpenny press to spread this news through a London still in ruins. What made matters worse, the sailors were more than half-mutinous, being paid with tickets not readily convertible into cash. Many of them actually deserted to the Dutch fleet, which made its leisurely way upstream, passing Upnor Castle, which had guns but no ammunition, till it was almost within reach of Chatham, where lay the royal navy. General Monk, who was the handy man of the period, and whose authority was always invoked when the king he had restored was in greater trouble than usual, had hastily collected what troops he could muster, and marched to protect Chatham; but what were wanted were ships, not troops. The Dutch had no mind to land, and after firing three warships (the *Royal James*, the *Royal Oak*, and the *London*), and capturing the *Royal Charles*, "they thought they had done enough, and made use of the ebb to carry them back again."[1] These events occupied the tenth to the fifteenth of June, and for the impression they produced on Marvell's mind we are not dependent upon his restrained letters to his constituents, but can turn to his longest rhymed satire, which is believed to have been first printed, anonymously of course, as a broadsheet in August 1667.

This poem is called *The Last Instructions to a Painter about the Dutch Wars*, 1667. The title was derived from Waller's panegyric poem on the occasion of the Duke of York's victory over the Dutch on the 3rd of June 1665, when Opdam, the Dutch admiral, was blown up with his ship.[2] Sir John Denham, a brother satirist of Marvell's, and with as good an excuse for hating the Duke of York as this world affords, had seized upon the same idea and published four satirical poems on these same Dutch Wars, entitled *Directions to a Painter* (see *Poems on Affairs of State*, 1703, vol. i.).

Marvell's satire, which runs to 900 lines, is essentially a House of Commons poem, and could only have been written by a member. It is intensely "lobbyish" and "occasional." To understand its allusions, to appreciate its "pain-giving" capacity to the full, is now impossible. Still, the reader of Clarendon's *Life*, Pepys's *Diary*, and Burnet's *History*, to name only popular books, will have no difficulty in entering into the spirit of the performance. As a poem it is rough in execution, careless, breathless. A rugged style was then in vogue. Even Milton could write his lines to the Cambridge Carrier somewhat in this manner. Marvell has nothing of the magnificence of Dryden, or of the finished malice of Pope. He plays the part, and it is sincerely played, of the old, honest member of Parliament who loves his country and hates rogues and speaks right out, calling spades spades and the king's women what they ought to be called. He is conversational, and therefore coarse. The whole history of the events that resulted in the national disgrace is told.

"The close cabal marked how the Navy eats
And thought all lost that goes not to the cheats;
So therefore secretly for peace decrees,
Yet for a War the Parliament would squeeze,

And fix to the revenue such a sum
Should Goodricke silence and make Paston dumb....
Meantime through all the yards their orders were
To lay the ships up, cease the keels begun.
The timber rots, the useless axe does rust,
The unpractised saw lies buried in the dust,
The busy hammer sleeps, the ropes untwine."

Parliament is got rid of to the joy of Clarendon.

"Blither than hare that hath escaped the hounds,
The house prorogued, the chancellor rebounds.
What frosts to fruits, what arsenic to the rat,
What to fair Denham mortal chocolate,[1]
What an account to Carteret, that and more,
A parliament is to the chancellor."

De Ruyter makes his appearance, and Monk

"in his shirt against the Dutch is pressed.
Often, dear Painter, have I sat and mused
Why he should be on all adventures used.
Whether his valour they so much admire,
Or that for cowardice they all retire,
As heaven in storms, they call, in gusts of state,
On Monk and Parliament—yet both do hate....
Ruyter, the while, that had our ocean curbed,
Sailed now amongst our rivers undisturbed;
Surveyed their crystal streams and banks so green,
And beauties ere this never naked seen."

His flags fly from the topmasts of his ships, but where is the enemy?

"So up the stream the Belgic navy glides,
And at Sheerness unloads its stormy sides."

Chatham was but a few miles further up.

"There our sick ships unrigged in summer lay,
Like moulting fowl, a weak and easy prey,
For whose strong bulk earth scarce could timber find,
The ocean water, or the heavens wind.
Those oaken giants of the ancient race,

That ruled all seas, and did our channel grace;
The conscious stag, though once the forest's dread,
Flies to the wood, and hides his armless head.
Ruyter forthwith a squadron doth untack;
They sail securely through the river's track.
An English pilot too (O, shame! O, sin!)
Cheated of 's pay, was he that showed them in."

The chain at Gillingham is broken, to the dismay of Monk, who

"from the bank that dismal sight does view;
Our feather gallants, who came down that day
To be spectators safe of the new play,
Leave him alone when first they hear the gun,
(Cornbury,[1] the fleetest) and to London run.
Our seamen, whom no danger's shape could fright,
Unpaid, refuse to mount their ships for spite,
Or to their fellows swim on board the Dutch,
Who show the tempting metal in their clutch."

Upnor Castle avails nought.

"And Upnor's Castle's ill-deserted wall
Now needful does for ammunition call."

The *Royal Charles* is captured before Monk's face.

"That sacred Keel that had, as he, restored
Its excited sovereign on its happy board,
Now a cheap spoil and the mean victor's slave
Taught the Dutch colours from its top to wave."

Horrors accumulate.

"Each doleful day still with fresh loss returns,
The loyal *London* now a third time burns,
And the true *Royal Oak* and *Royal James*,
Allied in fate, increase with theirs her flames.
Of all our navy none shall now survive,
But that the ships themselves were taught to dive,
And the kind river in its creek them hides.
Freighting their pierced keels with oozy tides."

The situation was indeed serious enough. One wiseacre in command in London declared his belief that the Tower was no longer "tenable."

"And were not Ruyter's maw with ravage cloyed,
Even London's ashes had been then destroyed."

But the Dutch admiral returns the way he came.

"Now nothing more at Chatham's left to burn,
The Holland squadron leisurely return;
And spite of Ruperts and of Albemarles,
To Ruyter's triumph led the captive *Charles*.
The pleasing sight he often does prolong,
Her mast erect, tough cordage, timber strong,
Her moving shape, all these he doth survey,
And all admires, but most his easy prey.
The seamen search her all within, without;
Viewing her strength, they yet their conquest doubt;
Then with rude shouts, secure, the air they vex,
With gamesome joy insulting on her decks.
Such the feared Hebrew captive, blinded, shorn,
Was led about in sport, the public scorn."

The poet then indulges himself in an emotional outburst.

"Black day, accursed! on thee let no man hail
Out of the port, or dare to hoist a sail,
Or row a boat in thy unlucky hour!
Thee, the year's monster, let thy dam devour,
And constant Time, to keep his course yet right,
Fill up thy space with a redoubled night.
When agèd Thames was bound with fetters base,
And Medway chaste ravished before his face,
And their dear offspring murdered in their sight,
Thou and thy fellows saw the odious light.
Sad change, since first that happy pair was wed,
When all the rivers graced their nuptial bed;
And father Neptune promised to resign
His empire old to their immortal line;
Now with vain grief their vainer hopes they rue,
Themselves dishonoured, and the gods untrue;
And to each other, helpless couple, moan,
As the sad tortoise for the sea does groan:

But most they for their darling Charles complain,
And were it burned, yet less would be their pain.
To see that fatal pledge of sea-command,
Now in the ravisher De Ruyter's hand,
The Thames roared, swooning Medway turned her tide,
And were they mortal, both for grief had died."

A scapegoat had, of course, to be at once provided. He was found in Mr. Commissioner Pett, the most skilful shipbuilder of the age.

"After this loss, to relish discontent,
Some one must be accused by Parliament.
All our miscarriages on Pett must fall,
His name alone seems fit to answer all.
 Whose counsel first did this mad war beget?
Who all commands sold through the navy? Pett.
Who would not follow when the Dutch were beat?
Who treated out the time at Bergen? Pett.
Who the Dutch fleet with storms disabled met?
And, rifling prizes, them neglect? Pett.
Who with false news prevented the Gazette?
The fleet divided? writ for Rupert? Pett.
Who all our seamen cheated of their debt,
And all our prizes who did swallow? Pett.
Who did advise no navy out to set?
And who the forts left unprepared? Pett.
Who to supply with powder did forget
Languard, Sheerness, Gravesend, and Upnor? Pett.
Who all our ships exposed in Chatham net?
Who should it be but the fanatic Pett?"

This outburst can hardly fail to remind the reader of a famous outburst of Mr. Micawber's on the subject of Uriah Heep.

The satire concludes with the picture of the king in the dead shades of night, alone in his room, startled by loud noises of cannons, trumpets, and drums, and then visited by the ghost of his father.

"And ghastly Charles, turning his collar low,
The purple thread about his neck does show."

The pensive king resolves on Clarendon's disgrace, and on rising next morning seeks out Lady Castlemaine, Bennet, and Coventry, who give him the same advice. He knows them all three to be false to one another and to him, but is for the moment content to do what they wish.

I have omitted, in this review of a long poem, the earlier lines which deal with the composition of the House of Commons. All its parties are described, one after another—the old courtiers, the pension-hunters, the king's procurers, then almost a department of State.

"Then the Procurers under Prodgers filed
Gentlest of men, and his lieutenant mild
Bronkard, love's squire; through all the field arrayed,
No troop was better clad, nor so well paid."

Clarendon had his friends, soon sorely to be needed, and after them,

"Next to the lawyers, sordid band, appear,
Finch in the front and Thurland in the rear."

Some thirty-three members are mentioned by their names and habits. The Speaker, Sir Edward Turner, is somewhat unkindly described. Honest men are usually to be found everywhere, and they existed even in Charles the Second's pensionary Parliament:—

"Nor could all these the field have long maintained
But for the unknown reserve that still remained;
A gross of English gentry, nobly born,
Of clear estates, and to no faction sworn,
Dear lovers of their king, and death to meet
For country's cause, that glorious thing and sweet;
To speak not forward, but in action brave,
In giving generous, but in council grave;
Candidly credulous for once, nay twice;
But sure the devil cannot cheat them thrice."

No member of Parliament's library is complete without Marvell, who did not forget the House of Commons smoking-room:—

"Even iron Strangways chafing yet gave back
Spent with fatigue, to breathe awhile tabac."

Charles hastened to make peace with Holland. He was not the man to insist on vengeance or to mourn over lost prestige. De Ruyter had gone after suffering repulses at Portsmouth, Plymouth, and Torbay. Peace was concluded at Breda on the 21st of July. We gave up Poleroone. *Per contra* we gained a more famous place, New Amsterdam, rechristened New York in honour of the duke. All prisoners were to be liberated, and the Dutch, despite Sheerness and the *Royal Charles*, agreed to lower their flag to all British ships of war.

The fall, long pending, of Clarendon immediately followed the peace. Men's tempers were furious or sullen. Hyde had no more bitter, no more cruel enemy than Marvell. Why this was has not been discovered, but there was nothing too bad for Marvell not to believe of any member of Clarendon's household. All the scandals, and they were many and horrible, relating to Clarendon and his daughter, the Duchess of York, find a place in Marvell's satires and epigrams. To us Lord Clarendon is a grave and thoughtful figure, the statesman-author of *The History of the Rebellion and Civil Wars in England*, that famous, large book, loftily planned, finely executed, full of life and character and the philosophy of human existence; and of his own *Autobiography*, a production which, though it must, like Burnet's *History*, be read with caution, unveils to the reader a portion of that past which usually is as deeply shrouded from us as the future. If at times we are reminded in reading Clarendon's *Life* of the old steward in Hogarth's plate, who lifts up his hands in horror over the extravagance of his master, if his pedantry often irritates, and his love of place displeases, we recognise these but as the shades of the character of a distinguished and accomplished public servant. But to Marvell Clarendon was rapacious, ambitious, and corrupt, a man who had sold Oliver's Dunkirk to the French, and shared the price; who had selected for the king's consort a barren woman, so that his own damaged daughter might at least chance to become Queen of England, who hated Parliaments and hankered after a standing army, who took money for patents, who sold public offices, who was bribed by the Dutch about the terms of peace, who swindled the ruined cavaliers of the funds subscribed for their benefit, and had by these methods heaped together great wealth which he ostentatiously displayed. Even darker crimes than these are hinted at. That Marvell was wrong in his estimate of Clarendon's character now seems certain; Clarendon did not get a penny of the Dunkirk money. The case made against him by the House of Commons in their articles of impeachment was felt even at the time to be flimsy and incapable of proof, and in the many records that have come to light since Clarendon's day nothing has been discovered to give them support. And yet Marvell was a singularly well-informed member of Parliament, a shrewd, level-headed man of affairs, who knew Lord Clarendon in the way we know men we have to see on business matters, whose speeches we can listen to, and whose conduct we discuss and criticise. "Gently scan your brother-man" is a precept Marvell never took to heart; nor is the House of Commons a place where it is either preached or practised.

When Clarendon was well nigh at the height of his great unpopularity, he built himself a fine big house on a site given him by the king where now is Albemarle Street. Where did he get the money from? He employed, in building it, the stones of St. Paul's Cathedral. True, he bought the stones from the Dean and Chapter, but if the man you hate builds a great house out of the ruins of a church, is it likely that so trivial a fact as a cash payment for the materials is going to be mentioned? Splendid furniture and noble pictures were to be seen going into the new palace—the gifts, so it was alleged, of foreign ambassadors. What was the consideration for these donations? England's honour! Clarendon House was at once named Dunkirk House, Holland House, Tangiers House.

Here is Marvell upon it:—

UPON HIS HOUSE

"Here lie the sacred bones
Of Paul beguilèd of his stones:
Here lie golden briberies,
The price of ruined families;
The cavalier's debenture wall,
Fixed on an eccentric basis:
Here's Dunkirk-Town and Tangier-Hull,
The Queen's marriage and all,
The Dutchman's *templum pacis*."

Clarendon's fall was rapid. He knew the house of Stuart too well to place any reliance upon the king. Evelyn visited him on the 27th of August 1667 after the seals had been taken away from him, and found him "in his bed-chamber very sad." His enemies were numerous and powerful, both in the House of Commons and at Court, where all the buffoons and ladies of pleasure hated him, because—so Evelyn says—"he thwarted some of them and stood in their way." In November Evelyn called again and found the late Lord-Chancellor in the garden of his new-built palace, sitting in his gout wheel-chair and watching the new gates setting up towards the north and the fields. "He looked and spoke very disconsolately. After some while deploring his condition to me, I took my leave. Next morning I heard he was gone."[1]

The news was true; on Saturday, the 29th of November, he drove to Erith, and after a terrible tossing on the nobly impartial Channel the weary man reached Calais, and died seven years later in Rouen, having well employed his leisure in completing his history. His palace was sold for half what it cost to the inevitable Monk, Duke of Albemarle.

On the 3rd of December Marvell writes that the House, having heard that Lord Clarendon had "withdrawn," forthwith ordered an address to his Majesty "that care might be taken for securing all the sea ports lest he should pass there." Marvell adds grimly, "I suppose he will not trouble you at Hull." The king took good care that his late Lord-Chancellor should escape. An act of perpetual banishment was at once passed, receiving the royal assent on the 19th of December.

Marvell was kept very busy during the early months of 1668, inquiring, as our English fashion is, into the "miscarriages of the late war." The House more than once sat from nine in the morning till eight at night, finding out all it could. "What money, arising by the poll money, had been applied to the use of the war?" This was an awkward inquiry. The House voted that the not prosecuting the first victory of June 1665 was a miscarriage, and one of the greatest: a snub to the Duke of York. The not furnishing the Medway with a sufficient guard of ships, though the king had then 18,000 men in his pay, was another great miscarriage. The paying of the fleet with tickets, without money, was a third great miscarriage. All this time Oliver Cromwell's skull was grinning on its perch in Westminster Hall.

Besides the honour of England, that of Hull had to be defended by its member. A young Lieutenant Wise, one of the Hull garrison, had in some boisterous fashion affronted the corporation and the mayor. On this correspondence ensues; and Marvell waits upon the Duke of Albemarle, the head of the army, to obtain reparation.

"I waited yesterday upon my Lord General—and first presented your usual fee which the General accepted, but saying that it was unnecessary and that you might have bin pleased to spare it, and he should be so much more at liberty to show how voluntary and affectionate he was toward your corporation. I returned the civilest words I could coin on for the present, and rendered him your humble thanks for his continued patronage of you ... and told him that you had further sent him up a small tribute of your Hull liquor. He thanked you again for all these things which you might—he said—have spared, and added that if the greatest of your military officers should demean himself ill towards you, he would take a course with him."

A mealy-mouthed Lord-General drawing near his end.[1]

Wise was removed from the Hull garrison. The affronted corporation was not satisfied, and Marvell had to argue the point.

"And I hope, Sir, you will incline the Bench to consider whether I am able or whether it be fit for me to urge it beyond that point. Yet it is not all his (Wise's) Parliament men and relations that have wrought me in the least, but what I simply conceive as the state of things now to be possible and satisfactory. What would you have more of a soldier than to run away and have him cashiered as to any command in your garrison? The first he hath done and the second he must submit to. And I assure you whatsoever he was among you, he is here a kind of decrepit young gentleman and terribly crest-fallen."

The letter concludes thus:—

"For I assure you they use all the civility imaginable to you, and as we sat there drinking a cup of sack with the General, Colonel Legge[1] chancing to be present, there were twenty good things said on all hands tending to the good fame, reputation, and advantage of the Town, an occasion that I was heartily glad of."

Corporations may not have souls to save and bodies to kill, but evidently they have vanities to tickle.

In November 1669 the House is still busy over the accounts. Sir George Carteret was Treasurer of the Navy. Marvell refers to him in *The Last Instructions to a Painter* as:—

"Carteret the rich did the accountants guideAnd in ill English all the world defied."

The following letter of Marvell's gives an excellent account of House of Commons business, both how it is conducted, and how often it gets accidentally interrupted by other business unexpectedly cropping up:—

"*November 20, 1669.*

"GENTLEMEN, MY VERY WORTHY FRIENDS,—Returning after our adjournment to sit upon Wednesday, the House having heard what Sir G. Cartaret could say for himselfe, and he then commended to withdraw, after a considerable debate, put it to the question, whether he were guilty of misdemeanour upon the Commissioners first observation, the words of which were, That all monyes received by him out of His Majesty's Exchequer are by the privy seales assigned for particular services, but no such thing observed or specified in his payments, whereby he hath assumed to himselfe a liberty to make use of the King's treasure for other uses then is directed. The House dividing upon the question, the ayes went out, and wondered why they were kept out so extraordinary a time. The ayes proved 138 and the noes 129; and the reason of the long stay then appeared; the tellers for the ayes chanced to be very ill reckoners, so that they were forced to tell severall times over in the House, and when at last the tellers for the ayes would have agreed the noes to be 142, the noes would needs say that they were 143, whereupon those for the ayes would tell once more and then found the noes to be indeed but 129; and the ayes then coming in proved to be 138; whereas if the noes had been content with the first error of the tellers, Sir George had been quit upon that observation. This I have told you so minutely because it is the second fatall and ominous accident that hath fain out in the divisions about Sir G. Cartaret. Thursday was ordered for the second observation, the words of which are, Two hundred and thirty thousand seven hundred thirty and one thousand pounds thirteen shillings and ninepence, claimed as payd, and deposited for security of interest, and yet no distinct specification of time appears either on his receits or payments, whereby no judgment can be made how interest accrues; so that we cannot yet allow the same. But this day was diverted and wholy taken up by a speciall report orderd by the Committee for the Bill of Conventicles, that the House be informed of severall Conventicles in Westminster which might be of dangerous consequences. From hence arose much discourse; also of a report that Ludlow was in England, that Commonwealths-men flock about the town, and there were meetings said to be, where they talkt of New Modells of Government; so that the House ordered a Committee to receive informations both concerning Conventicles and these other dangerous meetings; and then entered a resolution upon their books without putting it to the question, That this House will adhere to His Majesty, and the Government of Church and State as now established, against all its enemyes. Friday having bin appointed, as I told you in my former letter, for the House to sit in a grand Committee upon the motion for the King's supply, was spent wholy in debate, whether they should do so or no, and concluded at last in a consent, that the sitting in a grand Committee upon the motion for the King's supply should be put of till Friday next, and so it was ordered. The reason of which kind of proceeding, lest you should thinke to arise from an indisposition of the House, I shall tell you as they appear to me, to have been the expectation of what Bill will come from the Lords in stead of that of ours which they threw out, and a desire to redresse and see thoroughly into the miscarriages of mony before any more should be granted. To-day the House hath bin upon the second observation, and after a debate till foure a'clock, have voted him guilty also of misdemeanor in that particular. The Commissioners are ordered to attend the House again on Munday, which is done constantly for the illustration of any matter in their report, wherein the House is not cleare. And to say the truth, the House receives great satisfaction from them, and shows them extraordinary respect. These are the things of principall notice since my last."

Carteret eventually was censured and suspended and dismissed.

The sudden incursion of religion during a financial debate is highly characteristic of the House of Commons.

Whilst Queen Elizabeth and her advisers did succeed in making some sort of a settlement of religion having regard to the questions of her time, the Restoration bishops, an inferior set of men, wholly failed. The repressive legislation that followed upon the Act of Uniformity, succeeded in establishing and endowing (with voluntary contributions) what is sometimes called, absurdly enough, Political Dissent. On points, not of doctrine, but of ceremony, and of church government, one half of the religiously-minded community were by oaths and declarations, and by employing the Sacrament of the Lord's Supper as "a picklock to a place," drawn out of the service of the State. Excluded from Parliament and from all corporate bodies, from grammar-schools and universities, English Dissent learned to live its own life, remote from the army, the navy, and the civil service, quite outside of what perhaps may be fairly called the main currents of the national life. Nonconformists venerated their own divines, were reared in their own academies and colleges, read their own books, went, when the modified law permitted it, to their own conventicles in back streets, and made it their boast that they had never entered their parish churches, for the upkeep of which they were compelled to subscribe—save for the purpose of being married. The nation suffered by reason of this complete severance. Trade excepted, there was no community of interest between Church and Dissent. Sobriety, gravity, a decent way of life, the sense of religious obligation (even when united with the habit of *extempore* prayer, and a hereditary disrespect for bishops' aprons), are national assets, as the expression now goes, which cannot be disregarded with impunity.

The Conventicle Act Marvell refers to was a stringent measure, imposing pecuniary fines upon any persons of sixteen years of age or upwards who "under pretence of religion" should be present at any meeting of more than five persons, or more than those of the household, "in other manner than allowed by the Liturgy and practice of the Church of England." Heavier fines were imposed upon the preachers. The poet Waller, who was "nursed in Parliaments," having been first returned from Amersham in 1621, made a very sensible remark on the second reading: "Let them alone and they will preach against each other; by this Bill they will incorporate as being all under one calamity."[1] But by 144 to 78 the Bill was read, though it did not become law until the following session. An indignant Member of Parliament once told Cromwell that he would take the "sense" of the House against some proposal. "Very well," said Cromwell, "you shall take the 'sense' of the House, and I will take the 'nonsense,' and we will see who tells the most votes."

In February 1670 the king opened a new session, and in March Marvell wrote a private letter to a relative at Bordeaux, in which he "lends his mind out," after a fashion forbidden him in his correspondence with his constituents:—

"DEAR COUSIN,— ... You know that we having voted the King, before Christmas, four hundred thousand pounds, and no more; and enquiring severely into ill management, and being ready to adjourn ourselves till February, his Majesty, fortified by some undertakers of the meanest of our House, threw up all as nothing, and prorogued us from the first of December till the fourteenth of February. All that interval there was great and numerous caballing among the courtiers. The King also all the while examined at council the reports from the Commissioners of Accounts, where they were continually discountenanced, and treated rather as offenders than judges. In this posture we met, and the King, being exceedingly necessitous for money, spoke to us *stylo minaci et imperatorio*; and told us the inconveniences which would fall on the nation by want of a supply, should not ly at his door; that we must not revive any discord betwixt the Lords and us; that he himself had examined the accounts, and found every penny to have been employed in the war; and he recommended the Scotch union. The Garroway party appeared with the usual vigour, but the country gentlemen appeared not in their true number the first day: so, for want of seven voices, the first blow was against them. When we began to talk of the Lords, the King sent for us alone, and recommended a rasure of all proceedings. The same thing you know that we proposed at first. We presently ordered it, and went to tell him so the same day, and to thank him. At coming down, (a pretty ridiculous thing!) Sir Thomas Clifford carryed Speaker and Mace, and all members there, into the King's cellar, to drink his health. The King sent to the Lords more peremptoryly, and they, with much grumbling, agreed to the rasure. When the Commissioners of Accounts came before us, sometimes we heard them *pro formâ*, but all falls to dirt. The terrible Bill against Conventicles is sent up to the Lords; and we and the Lords, as to the Scotch busyness, have desired the King to name English Commissioners to treat, but nothing they do to be valid, but on a report to Parliament, and an act to confirm. We are now, as we think, within a week of rising. They are making mighty alterations in the Conventicle Bill (which, as we sent up, is the quintessence of arbitrary malice), and sit whole days, and yet proceed but by inches, and will, at the end, probably affix a Scotch clause of the King's power in externals. So the fate of the Bill is uncertain, but must probably pass, being the price of money. The King told some eminent citizens, who applyed to him against it, that they must address themselves to the Houses, that he must not disoblige his friends; and if it had been in the power of their friends, he had gone without money. There is a Bill in the Lords to encourage people to buy all the King's fee-farm rents; so he is resolved once more to have money enough in his pocket, and live on the common for the future. The great Bill begun in the Lords, and which makes more ado than ever any Act in this Parliament did, is for enabling Lord Ros, long since divorced in the spiritual court, and his children declared illegitimate by Act of Parliament, to marry again. Anglesey and Ashly, who study and know their interests as well as any gentlemen at court, and whose sons have married two sisters of Ros, inheritrixes if he has no issue, yet they also drive on the Bill with the greatest vigour. The King is for the Bill: the Duke of York, and all the Papist Lords, and all the Bishops, except Cosins, Reynolds, and Wilkins, are against it. They sat all Thursday last, without once rising, till almost ten at night, in most solemn and memorable debate, whether it should be read the second time, or thrown out. At last, at the question, there were forty-two persons and six proxys against it, and forty-one persons and fifteen proxys for it. If it had not gone for it, the Lord Arlington had a power in his pocket from the King to have nulled the proxys, if it had been to the purpose. It was read the second time yesterday, and, on a long debate whether it should be committed, it went for the Bill by twelve odds, in persons and proxys. The Duke of York, the bishops, and the rest of the party, have entered their protests, on the first day's debate, against it. Is not this fine work? This Bill must come down to us. It is my opinion that Lauderdale at one ear talks to the King of Monmouth, and Buckingham at the other of a new Queen. It is also my opinion that the King was never since his coming in, nay, all things considered, no King since the Conquest, so absolutely powerful at home, as he is at the present; nor any Parliament, or places, so certainly and constantly supplyed with men of the same temper. In such a conjuncture, dear Will, what probability is there of my doing any thing to the purpose? The King would needs take the Duke of Albemarle out of his son's hand to bury him at his own charges. It is almost three months, and he yet lys in the dark unburyed, and no talk of him. He left twelve thousand pounds a year, and near two hundred thousand pounds in money. His wife dyed some twenty days after him; she layed in state, and was buryed, at her son's expence, in Queen Elizabeth's Chapel. And now,

"Disce, puer, virtutem ex me verumque laborem,
Fortunam ex aliis.

"March 21, 1670."

This remarkable letter lets us into many secrets.

The Conventicle Bill is "the price of money." The king's interest in the Roos divorce case was believed to be due to his own desire to be quit of a barren and deserted wife.[1] Our most religious king had nineteen bastards, but no lawful issue. It may seem strange that so high a churchman as Bishop Cosin should have taken the view he did, but Cosin had a strong dash of the layman in his constitution, and was always an advocate of divorce, with permission to re-marry, in cases of adultery.

A further and amending Bill for rebuilding the city was before the House—one of eighty-four clauses, "the longest Bill, perhaps, that ever past in Parliament," says Marvell; but the Roos Divorce Bill and the Conventicle Bill proved so exciting in the House of Lords that they had little time for anything else. Union with Scotland, much desired by the king, but regarded with great suspicion by all Parliamentarians, fell flat, though Commissioners were appointed.

The Conventicle Bill passed the Lords, who tagged on to it a proviso Marvell refers to in his next letter, which the Lower House somewhat modified by the omission of certain words. Lord Roos was allowed to re-marry. The big London Bill got through.

Another private letter of Marvell's, of this date, is worth reading:—

"DEAREST WILL,—I wrote to you two letters, and payd for them from the posthouse here at Westminster; to which I have had no answer. Perhaps they miscarryed. I sent on an answer to the only letter I received from Bourdeaux, and having put it into Mr. Nelthorp's hand, I doubt not but it came to your's. To proceed. The same day (March 26th letter) my letter bore date, there was an extraordinary thing done. The King, about ten o'clock, took boat, with Lauderdale only, and two ordinary attendants, and rowed awhile as towards the bridge, and soon turned back to the Parliament stairs, and so went up into the House of Lords, and took his seat. Almost all of them were amazed, but all seemed so; and the Duke of York especially was very much surprized. Being sat, he told them it was a privilege he claimed from his ancestors to be present at their deliberations. That therefore, they should not, for his coming, interrupt their debates, but proceed, and be covered. They did so. It is true that this has been done long ago, but it is now so old, that it is new, and so disused, that at any other but so bewitched a time as this, it would have been looked on as an high usurpation, and breach of privilege. He indeed sat still, for the most part, and interposed very little; sometimes a word or two. But the most discerning opinion was, that he did herein as he rowed for having had his face first to the Conventicle Bill, he turned short to the Lord Ross's. So that, indeed, it is credible, the King, in prospect of diminishing the Duke of York's influence in the Lord's House, in this, or any future matter, resolved, and wisely enough at present, to weigh up and lighten the Duke's efficacy, by coming himself in person. After three or four days continuance, the Lords were very well used to the King's presence, and sent the Lord Steward and Lord Chamberlain, to him, when they might wait, as an House on him, to render their humble thanks for the honour he did them. The hour was appointed them, and they thanked him, and he took it well. So this matter, of such importance on all great occasions, seems riveted to them, and us, for the future, and to all posterity. Now the Lord Ross's Bill came in order to another debate, and the King present. Nevertheless the debate lasted an entire day; and it passed by very few voices. The King has ever since continued his session among them, and says it is better than going to a play. In this session the Lords sent down to us a proviso[1] for the King, that would have restored him to all civil or ecclesiastical prerogatives which his ancestors had enjoyed at any time since the Conquest. There was never so compendious a piece of absolute universal tyranny. But the Commons made them ashamed of it, and retrenched it. The Parliament was never embarrassed, beyond recovery. We are all venal cowards, except some few. What plots of State will go on this interval I know not. There is a new set of justices of peace framing through the whole kingdom. The governing cabal, since Ross's busyness, are Buckingham, Lauderdale, Ashly, Orrery, and Trevor. Not but the other cabal too have seemingly sometimes their turn. Madam,[1] our King's sister, during the King of France's progress in Flanders, is to come as far as Canterbury. There will doubtless be family counsels then. Some talk of a French Queen to be then invented for our King. Some talk of a sister of Denmark; others of a good virtuous Protestant here at home. The King disavows it; yet he has sayed in publick, he knew not why a woman may not be divorced for barrenness, as a man for impotency. The Lord Barclay went on Monday last for Ireland, the King to Newmarket. God keep, and increase you, in all things.—Yours, etc.

"*April 14, 1670.*"

[77:1] Clarendon's *Life*, vol. ii. p. 442.

[79:1] The clerks, however, only *counted* the members who voted, and kept no record of their *names*. Mr. Gladstone remembered the alteration being made in 1836, and how unpopular it was. The change was a greater revolution than the Reform Bill. See *The Unreformed House of Commons* by Edward Posselt, vol. i. p. 587.

[79:2]

"And a Parliament had lately met
Without a single Bankes."—*Praed.*

[82:1] See Dr. Halley's *Lancashire—its Puritanism and Nonconformity*, vol. ii. pp. 1-140, a most informing book.

[88:1] Clarendon's *History*, vol. vi. p. 249.

[90:1] An Historical Poem.—Grosart, vol. i. p. 343.

[92:1] Macaulay's *History*, vol. i. p. 154.

[95:1] I am acquainted with the romantic story which would have us believe that Lady Fauconberg, foretelling the time to come, had caused some other body than her father's to be buried in the Abbey (see *Notes and Queries*, 5th October 1878, and Waylen's *House of Cromwell*, p. 341).

[96:1] See *The Unreformed House of Commons*, by Edward Porritt, vol. i. p. 51. Marvell's old enemy, Parker, Bishop of Oxford, in his *History of his own Time*, composed after Marvell's death, reviles his dead antagonist for having taken this payment which, the bishop says, was made by a custom which "had a long time been antiquated and out of date." "Gentlemen," says the bishop, "despised so vile a stipend," yet Marvell required it "for the sake of a bare subsistence, although in this mean poverty he was nevertheless haughty and insolent." In Parker's opinion poor men should be humble.

[98:1] *Parliamentary History*, vol. iv., App. No. III.

[104:1] Mr. Gladstone's testimony is that no real improvement was effected until within the period of his own memory. 'Our services were probably without a parallel in the world for their debasement.' (See *Gleanings*, vi. p. 119.)

[106:1] There is a copy in the library of the *Athenæum*, London: "A Relation of Three Embassies from his sacred Majestie Charles II. to the Great Duke of Muscovie, the King of Sweden, and the King of Denmark. Performed by the Right Ho[ble] the Earle of Carlisle in the Years 1663 and 1664. Written by an Attendant on the Embassies, and published with his Lordship's approbation. London. Printed for John Starkie at the Miter in Fleet Street, near Temple Barr, 1669."

[109:1] "I have mentioned the dignity of his manners.... He was at his very best on occasion of Durbars, investitures, and the like.... It irritated him to see men giggling or jeering instead of acting their parts properly."—*Life of Lord Dufferin*, vol. ii. p. 317.

[116:1] *Hist. MSS. Com., Portland Papers*, vol. iii. p. 296.

[116:2] See above, vol. iii. p. 294.

[118:1] Sir Walter Besant doubted this. See his *London*.

[123:1] Mr. Goldwin Smith says this was the first pitched battle between Protection and Free Trade in England.—*The United Kingdom*, vol. ii. p. 25.

[126:1] Being curious to discover whether no "property" man raised his voice against these measures, I turned to that true "home of lost causes," the

Protests of the House of Lords; and there, sure enough, I found one solitary peer, Henry Carey, Earl of Dover, entering his dissent to both Bills—to the Judicature Bill because of the unlimited power given to the judges, to the Rebuilding Bill because of the exorbitant powers entrusted to the Lord Mayor and Aldermen to give away or dispose of the property of landlords.

[128:1] Clarendon's *Life*, vol. iii. p. 796.

[129:1] Clarendon's *Life*, vol. iii. p. 798.

[129:2] "Instructions to a Painter for the drawing of the Posture and Progress of His Majesty's forces at Sea under the command of His Highness Royal: together with the Battel and Victory obtained over the Dutch, June 3, 1665."—Waller's *Works*, 1730, p. 161.

[130:1] Sir John Denham's wife was reported to have been poisoned by a dish of chocolate, at the bidding of the Duchess of York.

[131:1] Clarendon's eldest son.

[139:1] It is disconcerting to find Evelyn recording this, his last visit to Clarendon, in his Diary under date of the 9th December, by which time the late Chancellor was in Rouen. One likes notes in a diary to be made contemporaneously and not "written-up" afterwards. Evelyn makes the same kind of mistake about Cromwell's funeral, misdating it a month.

[140:1] The duke died in 1670 and had a magnificent funeral on the 30th of April. See *Hist. MSS. Com., Duke of Portland's Papers*, vol. iii. p. 314. His laundress-Duchess did not long survive him.

[141:1] Afterwards Lord Dartmouth, a great friend of James the Second, but one who played a dubious part at the Revolution.

[145:1] The poet Waller was one of the wittiest speakers the House of Commons has ever known.

[148:1] For a full account of this remarkable case, see Clarendon's *Life*, iii. 733-9.

[149:1] "Provided, etc., that neither this Act nor anything therein contained shall extend to invalidate or avoid his Majesty's supremacy in ecclesiastical affairs [or to destroy any of his Majesty's rights powers or prerogatives belonging to the Imperial Crown of this realm or at any time exercised by himself or any of his predecessors Kings or Queens of England] but that his Majesty his heirs and successors may from time to time and at all times hereafter exercise and enjoy all such powers and authorities aforesaid as fully and amply as himself or any of his predecessors have or might have done the same anything in this Act (or any other law statute or usage to the contrary) notwithstanding." The words in brackets were rejected by the Commons. See *Parliamentary History*, iv. 446-7.

[150:1] Madame's business is now well known. The secret Treaty of Dover was the result of this visit.

CHAPTER V

"THE REHEARSAL TRANSPROSED"

It is never easy for ecclesiastical controversy to force its way into literature. The importance of the theme will be questioned by few. The ability displayed in its illumination can be denied by none. It is the temper that usually spoils all. A collection in any way approaching completeness, of the pamphlets this contention has produced in England, would contain tens of thousands of volumes; full of curious learning and anecdotes, of wide reading and conjecture, of shrewdness and wit; yet these books are certainly the last we would seek to save from fire or water. Could they be piled into scales of moral measurement a single copy of the *Imitatio*, of the *Holy Dying*, of the *Saint's Rest*, would outweigh them all. Man may not be a religious animal, but he recognises and venerates the spirit of religion whenever he perceives it, and it is a spirit which is apt to evaporate amidst the strife of rival wits. Who can doubt the sincerity of Milton, when he exclaimed with the sad prophet Jeremy, "Woe is me my Mother that thou hast borne me a man of strife and contention."

Marvell's chief prose work, the two parts of *The Rehearsal Transprosed*, is a very long pamphlet indeed, composed by way of reply to certain publications of Samuel Parker, afterwards Bishop of Oxford. Controversially Marvell's book was a great success.[1] It amused the king, delighted the wits, was welcomed, if not read, by the pious folk whose side it espoused, whilst its literary excellence was sufficient to win, in after years, the critical approval of Swift, whose style, though emphatically his own, bears traces of its master having given, I will not say his days and nights, but certainly some profitable hours, to the study of Marvell's prose.

Biographers of controversialists seldom do justice to the other side. Possibly they do not read it, and Parker has been severely handled by my predecessors. He was not an honour to his profession, being, perhaps, as good or as bad a representative of the seamy side of State Churchism as there is to be found. He was the son of a Puritan father, and whilst at Wadham lived by rule, fasting and praying. He took his degree in the early part of 1659, and migrating to Trinity came under the influence of Dr. Bathurst, then Senior Fellow, to whom, so he says in one of his dedications, "I owe my first rescue from the chains and fetters of an unhappy education."[2] Anything Parker did he did completely, and we next hear of him in London in 1665, a nobleman's chaplain, setting the table in a roar by making fun of his former friends, "a mimical way of drolling upon the puritans." "He followed the town-life, haunted the best companies and, to polish himself from any pedantic roughness, he read and saw the plays with much care and more preparing than most of the auditory." In 1667 the Archbishop of Canterbury, Dr. Sheldon, a very mundane person indeed, made Parker his chaplain, and three years later Archdeacon of Canterbury. He reached many preferments, so that, says Marvell, "his head swell'd like any bladder with wind and vapour." He had an active pen and a considerable range of subject. In 1670 he produced "A Discourse of Ecclesiastical Politie wherein the Authority of the Civil Magistrate over the Consciences of Subjects in Matters of External Religion is Asserted; The Mischiefs and Inconveniences of Toleration are represented and all Pretenses pleaded in behalf of *Liberty of Conscience* are fully answered." Some one instantly took up the cudgels in a pamphlet entitled *Insolence and Impudence Triumphant*, and the famous Dr. Owen also protested in *Truth and Innocence Vindicated*. Parker replied to Owen in *A Defence and Continuation of Ecclesiastical Politie*, and in the following year, 1672, reprinted a treatise of Bishop Bramholl's with a preface "shewing what grounds there are of Fears and Jealousies of Popery."

This was the state of the controversy when Marvell entered upon it with his *Rehearsal Transprosed*, a fantastic title he borrowed for no very good reasons from the farce of the hour, and a very good farce too, the Duke of Buckingham's *Rehearsal*, which was performed for the first time at the Theatre Royal on the 7th of November 1671, and printed early in 1672. Most of us have read Sheridan's *Critic* before we read Buckingham's *Rehearsal*, which is not the way to do justice to the earlier piece. It is a matter of literary tradition that the duke had much help in the composition of a farce it took ten years to make. Butler, Sprat, and Clifford, the Master of Charterhouse, are said to be co-authors. However this may be, the piece was a great success, and both Marvell and Parker, I have no doubt, greatly enjoyed it, but I cannot think the former was wise to stuff his plea for Liberty of Conscience so full as he did with the details of a farce. His doing so should, at all events, acquit him of the charge of being a sour Puritan. In the *Rehearsal* Bayes (Dryden), who is turned by Sheridan in his adaptation of the piece into Mr. Puff, is made to produce out of his pocket his book of *Drama Commonplaces*, and the play proceeds (*Johnson* and *Smith* being *Sheridan's* Dangle and Sneer):

"*Johnson. Drama Commonplaces!* pray what's that?

Bayes. Why, Sir, some certain helps, that we men of Art have found it convenient to make use of.

Johnson. How, Sir, help for Wit?

Bayes. I, Sir, that's my position. And I do here averr, that no man yet the Sun e'er shone upon, has parts sufficient to furnish out a Stage, except it be with the help of these my rules.

Johnson. What are those Rules, I pray?

Bayes. Why, Sir, my first Rule is the Rule of Transversion, or *Regula Duplex*, changing Verse into Prose, or Prose into Verse, *alternative* as you please.

Smith. How's that, Sir, by a Rule, I pray?

Bayes. Why, thus, Sir; nothing more easy when understood: I take a Book in my hand, either at home, or elsewhere, for that's all one, if there be any Wit in 't, as there is no Book but has some, I Transverse it; that is, if it be Prose, put it into Verse (but that takes up some time), if it be Verse, put it into Prose.

Johnson. Methinks, Mr. *Bayes*, that putting Verse into Prose should be called Transprosing.

Bayes. By my troth, a very good Notion, and hereafter it shall be so."

Marvell must be taken to have meant by his title that he saw some resemblance between Parker and Bayes, and, indeed, he says he does, and gives that as one of his excuses for calling Parker Bayes all through:—

"But before I commit myself to the dangerous depths of his Discourse which I am now upon the brink of, I would with his leave, make a motion; that instead of Author I may henceforth indifferently well call him Mr. Bayes as oft as I shall see occasion. And that first because he has no name, or at least will not own it, though he himself writes under the greatest security, and gives us the first letters of other men's names before he be asked them. Secondly, because he is, I perceive, a lover of elegancy of style and can endure no man's tautologies but his own; and therefore I would not distaste him with too frequent repetition of one word. But chiefly because Mr. Bayes and he do very much symbolise, in their understandings, in their expressions, in their humour, in their contempt and quarrelling of all others, though of their own profession."

But justice must be done even to Parker before handing him over to the Tormentor. What were his positions? He was a coarse-fibred, essentially irreligious fellow, the accredited author of the reply to the question "What is the best body of Divinity?" "That which would help a man to keep a Coach and six horses," but he is a lucid and vigorous writer, knowing very well that he had to steer his ship through a narrow and dangerous channel, avoiding Hobbism on the one side and tender consciences on the other. Each generation of State Churchmen has the same task. The channel remains to-day just as it ever did, with Scylla and Charybdis presiding over their rocks as of old. Hobbes's *Leviathan* appeared in 1651, and in 1670 both his philosophy and his statecraft were fashionable doctrine. All really pious people called Hobbes an Atheist. Technically he was nothing of the sort, but it matters little what he was technically, since no plain man who can read can doubt that Hobbes's enthronement of the State was the dethronement of God:—

"Seeing then that in every Christian commonwealth the civil sovereign is the supreme factor to whose charge the whole flock of his subjects is commuted, and consequently that it is by his authority that all other pastors are made and have power to teach and perform all other pastoral offices, it followeth also that it is from the civil sovereign that all other pastors derive their right of teaching, preaching and other functions pertaining to that office, and that they are but his ministers in the same way as the magistrates of towns, judges in Court of Justice and commanders of assizes are all but ministers of him that is the magistrate of the whole commonwealth, judge of all causes and commander of the whole militia, which is always the Civil Sovereign. And the reason hereof is not because they that teach, but because they that are to learn, are his subjects."—(*The Leviathan*, Hobbes's *English Works* (Molesworth's Edition), vol. iii. p. 539.)

Hobbes shirks nothing, and asks himself the question, What if a king, or a senate or other sovereign person forbid us to believe in Christ? The answer given is, "such forbidding is of no effect; because belief and unbelief never follow men's commands." But suppose "we be commanded by our lawful prince to say with our tongue we believe not, must we obey such command?" Here Hobbes a little hesitates to say outright "Yes, you must"; but he does say "whatsoever a subject is compelled to do in obedience to his own Sovereign, and doth it not in order to his own mind, but in order to the laws of his country, that action is not his, but his Sovereign's—nor is it that he in this case denieth Christ before men, but his Governor and the law of his country." Hobbes then puts the case of a Mahomedan subject of a Christian Commonwealth who is required under pain of death to be present at the Divine Service of the Christian Church—what is he to do? If, says Hobbes, you say he ought to die, then you authorise all private men to disobey their princes in maintenance of their religion, true or false, and if you say the Mahomedan ought to obey, you admit Hobbes's proposition and ought to consent to be yourself bound by it. (See Hobbes's *English Works*, iii. 493.)

The Church of England, though anxious both to support the king and suppress the Dissenters, could not stomach Hobbes; but if it could not, how was it to deal with Hobbes's question, "if it is *ever* right to disobey your lawful prince, who is to determine *when* it is right?"

Parker seeks to grapple with this difficulty. He disowns Hobbes.

"When men have once swallowed this principle, that Mankind is free from all obligations antecedent to the laws of the Commonwealth, and that the Will of the Sovereign Power is the only measure of Good and Evil, they proceed suitably to its consequences to believe that no Religion can obtain the force of law till it is established as such by supreme authority, that the Holy Scriptures were not laws to any man till they were enjoyn'd by the

Christian Magistrate, and that if the Sovereign Power would declare the Alcoran to be Canonical Scripture, it would be as much the Word of God as the Four Gospels. (See *Hobbes*, vol. iii. p. 366.) So that all Religions are in reality nothing but Cheats and impostures to awe the common people to obedience. And therefore although Princes may wisely make use of the foibles of Religion to serve their own turns upon the silly multitude, yet 'tis below their wisdom to be seriously concerned themselves for such fooleries." (Parker's *Ecc. Politie*, p. 137.)

As against this fashionable Hobbism, Parker pleads Conscience.

"When anything that is apparently and intrinsically evil is the Matter of a Human Law, whether it be of a Civil or Ecclesiastical concern, here God is to be obeyed rather than Man."

He forcibly adds:—

"Those who would take off from the Consciences of Men all obligations antecedent to those of Human Laws, instead of making the power of Princes Supreme, Absolute and Uncontrollable, they utterly enervate all their authority, and set their subjects at perfect liberty from all their commands. For if we once remove all the antecedent obligations of Conscience and Religion, Men will no further be bound to submit to their laws than only as themselves shall see convenient, and if they are under no other restraint it will be their wisdom to rebel as oft as it is their interest." (*Ecc. Politie*, pp. 112-113.)

But though when dealing with Hobbes, Parker thinks fit to assert the claims of conscience so strongly, when he has to grapple with those who, like the immortal author of *The Pilgrim's Progress*, "devilishly and perniciously abstained from coming to Church," and upheld "unlawful Meetings and Conventicles," his tone alters, and it is hard to distinguish his position from that of the philosopher of Malmesbury.

Parker's argument briefly stated, and as much as possible in his own vigorous language, comes to this:

There is and always must be a competition between the prerogative of the Prince or State and that of Conscience, which on this occasion is defined as "every private man's own judgment and persuasion of things." "Do subjects rebel against their Sovereign? 'Tis Conscience that takes up arms. Do they murder Kings? 'Tis under the conduct of Conscience. Do they separate from the communion of the Church? 'Tis Conscience that is the Schismatick. Everything that a man has a mind to is his Conscience." (*Ecc. Politie*, p. 6.)

How is this competition to be resolved? Parker answers in exact language which would have met with John Austin's warm approval.

"The Supreme Government of every Commonwealth, wherever it is lodged, must of necessity be universal, absolute and uncontrollable. For if it be limited, it may be controlled, but 'tis a thick and palpable contradiction to call such a power supreme in that whatever controls it must as to that case be its Superior. And therefore affairs of Religion being so strongly influential upon affairs of State, they must be as uncontrollably subject to the Supreme Power as all other Civil concerns." (*Ecc. Politie*, p. 27.)

If the magistrate may make penal laws against swearing and blasphemy, why not as to rites and ceremonies of public worship? (39.) Devotion towards God is a virtue akin to gratitude to man; religion is a branch of morality. The Puritans' talk about grace is a mere imposture, (76) which extracts from Parker vehement language. What is there to make such a fuss about? he cries. Why cannot you come to Church? You are left free to *think* what you like. Your secret thoughts are your own, but living as you do in society, and knowing as you must how, unless the law interferes, "every opinion must make a sect, and every sect a faction, and every faction when it is able, a war, and every war is the cause of God, and the cause of God can never be prosecuted with too much violence" (16), why cannot you conform to a form of worship which, though it does not profess to be prescribed in all particulars, contains nothing actually forbidden in the Scriptures? What authority have Dissenters for singing psalms in metre? "Where has our Saviour or his Apostles enjoined a directory for public worship? What Scripture command is there for the *three* significant ceremonies of the Solemn League and Covenant, viz. that the whole congregation should take it (1) uncovered, (2) standing, (3) with their right hand lift up bare" (184), and so on.

In answer to the objection that the civil magistrate might establish a worship in its own nature sinful and sensual, Parker replies it is not in the least likely, and the risk must be run. "Our enquiry is to find out the best way of settling the world that the state of things admit of—if indeed mankind were infallible, this controversy were at an end, but seeing that all men are liable to errors and mistakes, and seeing that there is an absolute necessity of a supreme power in all public affairs, our question (I say) is, What is the most prudent and expedient way of settling them, not that possibly might be, but that really is. And this (as I have already sufficiently proved) is to devolve their management on the supreme civil power which, though it may be imperfect and liable to errors and mistakes, yet 'tis the least so, and is a much better way to attain public peace and tranquillity than if they were left to the ignorance and folly of every private man" (212).

I now feel that at least I have done Parker full justice, but as so far I have hardly given an example of his familiar style, I must find room for two or three final quotations. The thing Parker hated most in the world was a *Tender*

Conscience. He protests against the weakness which is content with passing penal laws, but does not see them carried out for fear of wounding these trumpery tender consciences. "Most men's minds or consciences are weak, silly and ignorant things, acted by fond and absurd principles and imposed upon by their vices and their passions." (7.) "However, if the obligation of laws must yield to that of a tender conscience, how impregnably is every man that has a mind to disobey armed against all the commands of his superiors. No authority shall be able to govern him farther than he himself pleases, and if he dislike the law he is sufficiently excused (268). A weak conscience is the product of a weak understanding, and he is a very subtil man that can find the difference between a tender head and a tender conscience (269). It is a glorious thing to suffer for a tender conscience, and therefore it is easy and natural for some people to affect some little scruples against the commands of authority, thereby to make themselves obnoxious to some little penalties, and then what godly men are they that are so ready to be punished for a good conscience" (278). "The voice of the publick law cannot but drown the uncertain whispers of a tender conscience; all its scruples are hushed and silenced by the commands of authority. It dares not whimper when that forbids, and the nod of a prince awes it into silence and submission. But if they dare to murmur, and their proud stomachs will swell against the rebukes of their superiors, then there is no remedy but the rod and correction. They must be chastised out of their peevishness and lashed into obedience (305). The doctor concludes his treatise with the words always dear to men of fluctuating opinions, 'What I have written, I have written'" (326).

Whilst Parker was writing this book in his snug quarters in the Archbishop's palace at Lambeth, Bunyan was in prison in Bedford for refusing to take the communion on his knees in his parish church; and Dr. Manton, who had been offered the Deanery of Rochester, was in the Gate House Prison under the Five Mile Act.

The first part of *The Rehearsal Transprosed*, though its sub-title is "Animadversions upon a late book intituled a Preface shewing what grounds there are of Fears and Jealousies of Popery," deals after Marvell's own fashion with all three of Parker's books, the *Ecclesiastical Politie*, the *Bramhall Preface*, and the *Defence of the Ecclesiastical Politie*. It is by no means so easy to give a fair notion of the *Rehearsal Transprosed* in a short compass, as it was of Parker's line of argument. The parson wrote more closely than the Member of Parliament. I cannot give a better description of Marvell's method than in Parker's own words in his preface to his *Reproof to the Rehearsal Transprosed*, which appeared in 1673 and gave rise to Marvell's second part:—

"When," writes Parker, "I first condemned myself to the drudgery of this Reply, I intended nothing but a serious prosecution of my Argument, and to let the World see that it is not reading Histories or Plays or Gazettes, nor going on pilgrimage to Geneva, nor learning French and Italian, nor passing the Alps, nor being a cunning Gamester that can qualify a man to discourse of Conscience and Ecclesiastical Policy; in that it is not capping our Argument with a story that will answer it, nor clapping an apothegm upon an assertion that will prove it, nor stringing up Proverbs and Similitudes upon one another that will make up a Coherent Discourse."

Allowing for bias this is no unfair account of Marvell's method, and it was just because this was Marvell's method that he succeeded so well in amusing the king and in pleasing the town, and that he may still be read by those who love reading with a fair measure of interest and enjoyment.

Witty and humorous men are always at a disadvantage except on the stage. The hum-drum is the style for Englishmen. Bishop Burnet calls Marvell "a droll," Parker, who was to be a bishop, calls him "a buffoon." Marvell is occasionally humorous and not infrequently carries a jest beyond the limits of becoming mirth; but he is more often grave. Yet when he is, his gravity was treated either as one of his feebler jokes or as an impertinence. But as it is his wit alone that has kept him alive he need not be pitied overmuch.

The substance of Marvell's reply to Parker, apart altogether from its by-play, is to be found in passages like the following:—

"Here it is that after so great an excess of wit, he thinks fit to take a julep and re-settle his brain and the government. He grows as serious as 'tis possible for a madman, and pretends to sum-up the whole state of the controversy with the Nonconformists. And to be sure he will make the story as plausible for himself as he may; but therefore it was that I have before so particularly quoted and bound him up with his own words as fast as such a Proteus could be pinion'd. For he is as waxen as the first matter, and no form comes amiss to him. Every change of posture does either alter his opinion or vary the expression by which we should judge of it; and sitting he is of one mind, and standing of another. Therefore I take myself the less concern'd to fight with a windmill like Quixote; or to whip a gig as boyes do; or with the lacqueys at Charing-Cross or Lincoln's-Inn-Fields to play at the Wheel of Fortune; lest I should fall into the hands of my Lord Chief-Justice, or Sir Edmond Godfrey. The truth is, in short, and let Bayes make more or less of it if he can, Bayes had at first built-up such a stupendous magistrat as never was of God's making. He had put all princes upon the rack to stretch them to his dimension. And as a straight line continued grows a circle, he had given them so infinite a power, that it was extended unto impotency. For though he found it not till it was too late in the cause, yet he felt it all along (which is the understanding of brutes) in the effect. For hence it is that he so often complains that princes know not aright that supremacy over consciences, to which they were so lately, since their deserting the Church of Rome, restored;

that in most Nations government was not rightly understood, and many expressions of that nature: whereas indeed the matter is, that princes have always found that uncontroulable government over *conscience* to be both unsafe and impracticable. He had run himself here to a stand, and perceived that there was a God, there was Scripture; the magistrate himself had a conscience, and must 'take care that he did not enjoyn things apparently evil.' But after all, he finds himself again at the same stand here, and is run up to the wall by an angel. God, and Scripture, and conscience will not let him go further; but he owns, that if the magistrate enjoyns things apparently evil, the subject may have liberty to remonstrate. What shall he do, then? for it is too glorious an enterprize to be abandoned at the first rebuffe. Why, he gives us a new translation of the Bible, and a new commentary! He saith, that tenderness of conscience might be allowed in a Church to be constituted, not in a Church constituted already. That tenderness of conscience and scandal are ignorance, pride, and obstinacy. He saith, the Nonconformists should communicate with him till they have clear evidence that it is evil. This is a civil way indeed of gaining the question, to perswade men that are unsatisfied, to be satisfied till they be dissatisfied. He threatens, he rails, he jeers them, if it were possible, out of all their consciences and honesty; and finding that will not do, he calls out the magistrate, tells him these men are not fit to live; there can be no security of government while they are in being. Bring out the pillories, whipping-posts, gallies (=galleys), rods, and axes (which are *ratio ultima cleri*, a clergyman's last argument, ay and his first too), and pull in pieces all the Trading Corporations, those nests of Faction and Sedition. This is a faithful account of the sum and intention of all his undertaking, for which, I confess, he was as pick'd a man as could have been employed or found out in a whole kingdome; but it is so much too hard a task for any man to atchieve, that no goose but would grow giddy with it."[1]

In reply to what Parker had written about the unreasonable fuss made by the Dissenters over the "two or three symbolical ceremonies" called sacraments, Marvell says:—

"They (the Nonconformists) complain that these things should be imposed on them with so high a penalty as want nothing of a sacramental nature but divine institution. And because a human institution is herein made of equal force to a divine institution therefore it is that they are aggrieved.... For without the sign of the Cross our Church will not receive any one in Baptism; as also without kneeling no man is suffered to come to the Communion.... But here, I say, then is their (the Nonconformists') main exception that things indifferent and that have no proper signature or significancy to that purpose should by command be made conditions of Church-communion. I have many times wished for peaceableness' sake that they had a greater latitude, but if, unless they should stretch their consciences till they tear again, they cannot conform, what remedy? For I must confess that Christians have a better right and title to the Church and to the ordinances of God there, than the Author hath to his surplice.... Bishop Bramhall saith, 'I do profess to all the world that the transforming of indifferent opinions into necessary articles of faith hath been that *insana laurus* or cursed bay tree, the cause of all our brawling and contention.' That which he saw in matter of doctrine, he would not discern in discipline.... It is true and very piously done that our Church doth declare that the kneeling at the Lord's Supper is not enjoined for adoration of those elements and concerning the other ceremonies as before. But the Romanists (from whom we have them and who said of old we would come to feed on their meat as well as eat of their porridge) do offer us here many a fair declaration and distinction in very weighty matters to which nevertheless the conscience of our Church hath not complyed. But in this particular matter of kneeling which came in first with the doctrine of transubstantiation, the Romish Church do reproach us with flat idolatry, in that we, not believing the real presence in the bread and wine, yet do pay to something or other the same adoration. Suppose the ancient pagans had declared to the primitive Christians that the offerings of some grains of incense was only to perfume the room—do you think the Christians would have palliated so far and colluded with their consciences? Therefore although the Church do consider herself so much as not to alter her mode unto the fashion of others, yet I cannot see why she ought to exclude those from communion whose weaker consciences cannot, for fear of scandal, step further."[1]

With Parker's thunders and threats of the authority of princes and states, Marvell deals more in the mood of a statesman than of a philosopher, more as a man of affairs than as a jurist. He deplores the ferocity of Parker's tone and that of a certain number of the clergy.

"Why is it," he asks, "that this kind of clergy should always be and have been for the most precipitate, brutish, and sanguinary counsels? The former Civil War cannot make them wise, nor his Majesty's happy return good-natured, but they are still for running things up unto the same extremes. The softness of the Universities where they have been bred, the gentleness of Christianity, in which they have been nurtured, hath but exasperated their nature, and they seem to have contracted no idea of wisdom but what they learnt at school—the pedantry of Whipping. For whether it be or no that the clergy are not so well fitted by education as others for political affairs I know not, though I should rather think they have advantage above others, and even if they would but keep to their Bibles, might make the best Ministers of State in the world; yet it is generally observed that things miscarry under their government. If there be any council more precipitate, more violent, more extreme than other, it is theirs. Truly, I think the reason that God does not bless them in affairs of State is because he never intended them for that employment."[1]

Of Archbishop Laud and Charles the First, Marvell says:—

"I am confident the Bishop studied to do both God and his Majesty good service; but alas, how utterly was he mistaken. Though so learned, so pious, so wise a man, he seem'd to know nothing beyond Ceremonies, Armenianism, and Mainwaring. With that he begun, with that ended, and thereby deform'd the whole reign of the best prince that ever wielded the English sceptre. For his late Majesty, being a prince truly pious and religious, was therefore the more inclined to esteem and favour the clergy. And thence, though himself of a most exquisite understanding, yet he could not trust it better than in their treatment. Whereas every man is best at his own post, and so the preacher in the pulpit."[2]

Kings, Marvell points out to Parker, must take wider views than parsons.

"'Tis not with them as with you. You have but one cure of souls, or perhaps two as being a nobleman's chaplain, to look after, and if you made conscience of discharging them as you ought, you would find you had work sufficient without writing your 'Ecclesiastical Policies.' But they are the incumbents of whole kingdoms, and the rectorship of the common people, the nobility, and even of the clergy. The care I say of all this rests on them, so that they are fain to condescend to many things for peace sake and the quiet of mankind that your proud heart would break before it would bend to. They do not think fit to require any thing that is impossible, unnecessary or wanton of their people, but are fain to consider the very temper of the climate in which they live, the constitution and laws under which they have been formerly bred, and upon all occasions to give them good words and humour them like children. They reflect upon the histories of former times and the present transactions to regulate themselves by in every circumstance.... They (Kings) do not think fit to command things unnecessary."[1]

These extracts, however fatal to Marvell's traditional reputation in the eighteenth century as a Puritan and a Republican, call for no apology.

An example of Marvell's Interludes ought to be given. There are many to choose from.

"There was a worthy divine, not many years dead, who in his younger time, being of a facetious and unlucky humour, was commonly known by the name of Tom Triplet; he was brought up at Paul's school under a severe master, Dr. Gill, and from thence he went to the University. There he took liberty (as 'tis usual with those that are emancipated from School) to tel tales and make the discipline ridiculous under which he was bred. But not suspecting the doctor's intelligence, coming once to town he went in full school to give him a visite and expected no less than to get a play day for his former acquaintances. But instead of that he found himself hors'd up in a trice, though he appeal'd in vain to the priviledges of the University, pleaded *adultus* and invoked the mercy of the spectators. Nor was he let down till the master had planted a grove of birch in his back-side for the terrour and publick example of all waggs that divulge the secrets of Priscian and make merry with their teachers. This stuck so with Triplet that all his life-time he never forgave the doctor, but sent him every New Year's tide an anniversary ballad to a new tune, and so in his turn avenged himself of his jerking pedagogue."[2]

Marvell's game of picquet with a parson plays such a part in Parker's *Reproof* to the *Rehearsal Transprosed* that it deserves to be mentioned:—

"'Tis not very many years ago that I used to play at picket; there was a gentleman of your robe, a dignitory of Lincoln, very well known and remembered in the ordinaries, but being not long since dead, I will save his name. Now I used to play pieces, and this gentleman would always go half-a-crown with me; and so all the while he sate on my hand he very honestly '*gave the sign*' so that I was always sure to lose. I afterwards discovered it, but of all the money that ever I was cheated of in my life, none ever vexed me so as what I lost by his occasion."[1]

There is no need to pursue the controversy further. It is still unsettled.

Parker's *Reproof*, published in 1673, is less argumentative and naturally enough more personal than the *Ecclesiastical Politie*. Any use I now make of it will be purely biographical. Let us see Andrew Marvell depicted by an angry parson—not in passages of mere abuse, as *e.g.* "Thou dastard Craven, thou Swad, thou Mushroom, thou coward in heart, word and deed, thou Judas, thou Crocodile"; for epithets such as these are of no use to a biographer—but in places where Marvell is at least made to sit for the portrait, however ill-natured.

"And if I would study revenge I could easily have requited you with the Novels of a certain Jack Gentleman, that was born of pure parents and bred among cabin-boys, and sent from school to the University and from the University to the Gaming Ordinaries, but the young man, being easily rooked by the old Gamesters, he was sent abroad to gain courage and experience, and beyond sea saw the Bears of Berne and the large race of Capons at Geneva, and a great many fine sights beside, and so returned home as accomplished as he went out, tries his fortune once more at the Ordinaries, plays too high for a gentleman of his private condition, and so is at length cheated of all at Picquet." ... "And now to conclude; is it not a sad thing that a well-bred and fashionable gentleman that has frequented Ordinaries, that has worn Perukes and Muffs and Pantaloons and was once Master of a Watch, that has travelled abroad and seen as many men and countries as the famous Vertuosi, Sorbier and Coriat, that has heard the City Lions roar, that has past the Alps and seen all the Tredescin rarities and old stones of Italy, that has sat in the Porphyric Chair at Rome, that can describe the methods of the Elections of Popes and tell stories of the tricks of Cardinals, that has been employed in Embassies abroad and acquainted with Intrigues of State at home, that has read Plays and Histories and Gazettes; that I say a Gentleman thus accomplished and embellished within and without and all over, should ever live to that unhappy dotage as at last to dishonour his grey hairs and his venerable age with such childish and impotent endeavours at wit and buffoonery."—(*Reproof*, pp. 270, 274-5.)[1]

Marvell was very little over fifty years of his age at this time, nor is Parker's portrait to be regarded as truthful in any other particular—yet something of a man's character may be discovered by noticing the way he is abused by those who want to abuse him.

Marvell, though no orator, or even debater, was the stuff of which controversialists are made. In a letter, printed in the Duke of Portland's papers, and dated May 3, 1673, he writes:—

"Dr. Parker will be out the next week. I have seen it—already three hundred and thirty pages and it will be much more. (It was five hundred twenty-eight pages.) I perceive by what I have read that it is the rudest book, one or other, that ever was published, I may say since the first invention of printing. Although it handles me so roughly, yet I am not at all amated by it. But I must desire the advice of some few friends to tell me whether it will be proper for me and in what way to answer it. However I will for mine own private satisfaction forthwith draw up an answer that shall have as much of spirit and solidity in it as my ability will afford and the age we live in will endure. I am, if I may say it with reverence, drawn in I hope by a good Providence to intermeddle on a noble and high argument. But I desire that all the discourse of my friends may run as if no answer ought to be expected to so scurrilous a book."—(*Hist. MSS. Comm., Portland Papers*, iii. 337.)

The title-page of the Second Part of the *Rehearsal Transprosed* is a curiosity:—

THE

REHEARSALL

TRANSPROS'D:

THE SECOND PART.

Occasioned by Two Letters: The first Printed
by a nameless Author, Intituled, A
Reproof, etc.

The Second Letter left for me at a Friends
House, Dated Nov. 3, 1673. Subscribed
J. G. and concluding with these words;
If thou darest to Print or Publish any
Lie or Libel against Doctor Parker, By
the Eternal God I will cut thy Throat.

Answered by ANDREW MARVEL.

LONDON,

Printed for Nathaniel Ponder at the Peacock
in Chancery Lane near Fleet-Street, 1673.

The *Second Part* is an exceedingly witty though too lengthy a performance. Marvell's "companion picture" of Parker is full of matter, and of the very spirit of the times. Some of it must be given:—

"But though he came of a good mother, he had a very ill sire. He was a man bred toward the Law, and betook himself, as his best practice, to be a sub-committee-man, or, as the stile ran, one of the Assistant Committee in Northamptonshire. In the rapine of that employment, and what he got by picking the teeth of his masters, he sustain'd himself till he had raked together some little estate. And then, being a man for the purpose, and that had begun his fortune out of the sequestration of the estates of the King's Party, he, to perfect it the more, proceeded to take away their lives; not in the hot and military way (which diminishes always the offence), but in the cooler blood and sedentary execution of an High Court of Justice. Accordingly he was preferr'd to be one of that number that gave sentence against the three Lords, Capel, Holland, and Hamilton, who were beheaded. By this learning in the Law he became worthy of the degree of a serjeant, and sometimes to go the Circuit, till for misdemeanor he was petition'd against. But for a taste of his abilities, and the more to reingratiate himself, he printed, in the year 1650, a very remarkable Book, called 'The Government of the People of England, precedent and present the same. *Ad subscribentes confirmandum, Dubitantes informandum, Opponentes convincendum*; and underneath *Multa videntur quae non sunt, multa sunt quae non videntur*. Under that ingraven two hands joyn'd, with the motto, *Ut uniamur*; and beneath a sheaf of arrows, with this device, *Vis unita fortior*; and to conclude, *Concordia parvae res crescunt discordia dilabuntur*.' A most hieroglyphical title, and sufficient to have supplied the mantlings and atchievements of the family! By these parents he was sent to Oxford, with intention to breed him up to the ministry. There in a short time he enter'd himself into the company of some young students who were used to fast and pray weekly together; but for their refection fed sometimes on broth, from whence they were commonly called Grewellers; only it was observed that he was wont still to put more graves than all the rest in his porridge. And after that he pick'd acquaintance not only with the brotherhood at Wadham Colledge, but with the sisterhood too, at another old Elsibeth's, one Elizabeth Hampton's, a plain devout woman, where he train'd himself up in hearing their sermons and prayers, receiving also the Sacrament in the house, till he had gain'd such proficience, that he too began to exercise in that Meeting, and was esteem'd one of the preciousest young men in the University. But when thus, after several years' approbation, he was even ready to have taken the charge, not of an 'admiring drove or heard,' as he now calls them, but of a flock upon him, by great misfortune the King came in by the miraculous providence of God, influencing the distractions of some, the good affections of others, and the weariness of all towards that happy Restauration, after so many sufferings, to his regal crown and dignity. Nevertheless he broke not off yet from his former habitudes; and though it were now too late to obviate this inconvenience, yet he persisted as far as in him was—that is, by praying, caballing, and discoursing—to obstruct the restoring of the episcopal government, revenues, and authority. Insomuch that, finding himself discountenanced on those accounts by the then Warden of Wadham, he shifted colledges to Trinity, and, when there, went away without his degree, scrupling, forsooth, the Subscription then required. From thence he came to London, where he spent a considerable time in creeping into all corners and companies, horoscoping up and down concerning the duration of the Government; not considering anything as best, but as most lasting and most profitable. And after having many times cast a figure, he at last satisfyed himself that the Episcopal Government would endure as long as this King lived; and from thence forward cast about how to be admitted into the Church of England, and find the highway to her preferments. In order to this he daily enlarged, not only his conversation, but his conscience, and was made free of some of the town-vices; imagining, like Muleasses King of Tunis (for I take witness that on all occasions I treat him rather above his quality than otherwise), that by hiding himself among the onions, he should escape being traced by his perfumes. Ignorant and mistaken man, that thought it necessary to part with any virtue to get a living; or that the Church of England did not require and incourage more sobriety than he could ever be guilty of; whereas it hath always been fruitful of men who, together with obedience to that discipline, have lived to the envy of the Nonconformists in their conversation, and without such could never either have been preserved so long, or after so long a dissipation have ever recover'd. But neither was this yet, in his opinion, sufficient; and therefore he resolv'd to try a shorter path, which some few men had trod not unsuccessfully; that is, to print a Book; if that would not do, a second; if not that, a third of an higher extraction, and so forward, to give experiment against their former party of a keen stile and a ductile judgment. His first proof-piece was in the year 1665, the *Tentamina Physico-Theologica*; a tedious transcript of his common-place book, wherein there is very little of his own, but the arrogance and the unparalleled censoriousness that he exercises over all other Writers. When he had cook'd up these musty collections, he makes his first invitation to his 'old acquaintance' my lord Archbishop of Canterbury, who had never seen before nor heard of him. But I must confess he furbishes-up his Grace in so glorious an Epistle, that had not my Lord been long since proof against the most spiritual flattery, the Dedication only, without ever reading the Book, might have serv'd to have fix'd him from that instant as his favourite. Yet all this I perceive did not his work, but his Grace was so unmindful, or rather so prudent, that the gentleman thought it necessary to spur-up again the next year with another new Book, to show more plainly what he would be at. This he dedicates to Doctor Bathurst; and to evidence from the very Epistle that he was ready to renounce that very education, the civility of which he is so tender of as to blame me for disordering it, he picks occasion to tell him: 'to your prevailing advice, Sir, do I owe my first rescue from the chains and fetters of an unhappy education.' But in the Book, which he calls 'A free and impartial Censure of the Platonick Philosophy' (censure 'tis sure to be, whatsoever he writes), he speaks out, and demonstrates himself ready and equipp'd to surrender not only the Cause, but betray his Party without making any conditions for them, and to appear forthwith himself in the head of the contrary interest. Which, supposing the dispute to be just, yet in him was so mercenary, that none would have descended to act his part but a divine of fortune. And even lawyers take themselves excused from being of counsel for the King himself, in a cause where they have been entertain'd and instructed by their client. But so flippant he was and forward in this book, that in despight of all chronology, he could introduce Plato to inveigh against Calvin, and from the Platoniques he could miraculously hook-in a Discourse against the Nonconformists. (*Cens. Plat. Phil.*, pp. 26, 27, 28, etc.) After this feat of activity he was ready to leap over the moon; no scruple of conscience could stand in his way, and no preferment seemed too high for him; for about this time, I find that having taken a turn at Cambridge to qualifie himself, he was received within doors to be my Lord Archbishop's other chaplain, and into some degree of favour; which, considering the difference of their humours and ages, was somewhat surprizing. But whether indeed, in times of heat and faction, the most temperate spirits may sometimes chance to take delight in one that is spightful, and make some use of him; or whether it be that even the most grave and serious persons do for relaxation divert themselves willingly by whiles with a creature that is unlucky, inimical, and gamesome,—so it was. And thenceforward the nimble gentleman danced upon bell-ropes, vaulted from steeple to steeple, and cut capers out of one dignity to another. Having thus dexterously stuck his groat in Lambeth wainscot, it may easily be conceived he would be unwilling to lose it; and therefore he concern'd himself highly, and even to jealousie, in upholding now that palace, which, if falling, he would out of instinct be the first should leave it. His Majesty about that time labouring to effect his constant promises of Indulgence to his people, the Author therefore walking with his own shadow in the evening, took a great fright lest all were agoe. And in this conceit being resolv'd to make good his figure, and that one government should not last any longer than the other, he set himself to write those dangerous Books which I have now to do with; wherein he first makes all that he will to be Law, and then whatsoever is Law to be Divinity."[1]

The Second Part is not all raillery. There is much wisdom in it and a trace of Machiavelli:—

"But because you are subject to misconstrue even true English, I will explain my self as distinctly as I can, and as close as possible, what is mine own opinion in this matter of the magistrate and government; that, seeing I have blamed you where I thought you blame-worthy, you may have as fair hold of me too, if you can find where to fix your accusation.

"The power of the magistrate does most certainly issue from the divine authority. The obedience due to that power is by divine command; and subjects are bound, both as men and as Christians, to obey the magistrate actively in all things where their duty to God intercedes not, and however passively, that is, either by leaving their countrey, or if they cannot do that (the magistrate, or the reason of their own occasions hindring them), then by suffering patiently at home, without giving the least publick disturbance. But the dispute concerning the magistrate's power ought to be superfluous; for that it is certainly founded upon his commission from God, and for the most part sufficiently fortified with all humane advantages. There are few soveraign princes so abridged, but that, if they be not contented, they may envy their own fortune. But the modester question (if men will needs be medling with matters above them) would be, how far it is advisable for a prince to exert and push the rigour of that power which no man can deny him; for princes, as they derive the right of succession from their ancestors, so they inherit from that ancient and illustrious extraction a generosity that runs in the blood above the allay of the rest of mankind. And being moreover at so much ease of honour and fortune, that they are free from the gripes of avarice and twinges of ambition, they are the more disposed to an universal benignity toward their subjects. What prince that sees so many millions of men, either labouring industriously toward his revenue, or adventuring their lives in his service, and all of them performing his commands with a religious obedience, but conceives at the same time a relenting tenderness over them, whereof others out of the narrowness of their minds cannot be capable? But whoever shall cast his eye thorow the history of all ages, will find that nothing has always succeeded better with princes then the clemency of government; and that those, on the contrary, who have taken the sanguinary course, have been unfortunate to themselves and the people, the consequences not being separable. For whether that royal and magnanimous gentleness spring from a propensity of their nature, or be acquired and confirmed by good and prudent consideration, it draws along with it all the effects of Policy. The wealth of a shepherd depends upon the multitude of his flock, the goodness of their pasture, and the quietness of their feeding; and princes, whose dominion over mankind resembles in some measure that of men over other creatures, cannot expect any considerable increase to themselves, if by continual terrour they amaze, shatter, and hare their people, driving them into woods, and running them upon precipices. If men do but compute how charming an efficacy one word, and more, one good action has from a superior upon those under him, it can scarce be reckon'd how powerful a magick there is in a prince who shall, by a constant tenour of humanity in government, go on daily gaining upon the affections of his people. There is not any privilege so dear, but it may be extorted from subjects by good usage, and by keeping them alwayes up in their good humour. I will not say what one prince may compass within his own time, or what a second, though surely much may be done; but it is enough if a great and durable design be accomplish'd in the third life; and supposing an hereditary succession of any three taking up still where the other left, and dealing still in that fair and tender way of management, it is impossible but that, even without reach or intention upon the prince's part, all should fall into his hand, and in so short a time the very memory or thoughts of any such thing as publick liberty would, as it were by consent, expire and be for ever extinguish'd. So that whatever the power of the magistrate be in the institution, it is much safer for them not to do that with the left hand which they may do with the right, nor by an extraordinary, what they may effect by the ordinary, way of government. A prince that goes to the top of his power is like him that shall go to the bottom of his treasure."[1]

And as for the "common people" he has this to say:—

"Yet neither do they want the use of reason, and perhaps their aggregated judgment discerns most truly the errours of government, forasmuch as they are the first, to be sure, that smart under them. In this only they come to be short-sighted, that though they know the diseases, they understand not the remedies; and though good patients, they are ill physicians. The magistrate only is authorized, qualified, and capable to make a just and effectual Reformation, and especially among the Ecclesiasticks. For in all experience, as far as I can remember, they have never been forward to save the prince that labour. If they had, there would have been no Wickliffe, no Husse, no Luther in history. Or at least, upon so notable an emergency as the last, the Church of Rome would then in the Council of Trent have thought of rectifying itself in good earnest, that it might have recover'd its ancient character; whereas it left the same divisions much wider, and the Christian people of the world to suffer, Protestants under Popish governors, Popish under Protestants, rather than let go any point of interested ambition."[2]

[152:1] "But the most virulent of all that writ against the sect was Parker, afterwards made Bishop of Oxford by King James: who was full of satirical vivacity and was considerably learned, but was a man of no judgment and of as little virtue, and as to religion rather impious: after he had for some years entertained the nation with several virulent books writ with much life, he was attacked by the liveliest droll of the age, who writ in a burlesque strain but with so peculiar and entertaining a conduct that from the King down to the tradesman his books were read with great pleasure, that not only humbled Parker but the whole party, for the author of the *Rehearsal Transprosed* had all the men of wit (or as the French phrase it all the laughers) on his side."— Burnet's *History of his Own Time*.

[152:2] See the dedication to *A Free and Impartial Censure of the Plutonick Philosophy*, by Sam Parker, A.M., Oxford 1666. Parker was a man of some taste, and I have in my small collection a beautifully bound copy of this treatise presented by the author to Seth Ward, then Bishop of Exeter, and afterwards of Salisbury.

[165:1] Grosart, vol. iii. pp. 145-8.

[166:1] Grosart, vol. iii. pp. 155-9.

[167:1] Grosart, vol. iii. pp. 170, 210-1.

[167:2] Grosart, vol. iii. p. 211.

[168:1] Grosart, vol. iii. p. 171.

[168:2] Grosart, vol. iii. p. 63.

[169:1] Grosart, vol. iii. p. 198.

[170:1] For a still more unfriendly sketch of Andrew Marvell by the same spiteful hand, see Parker's *History of his Own Time*, a posthumous work, first published in Latin in 1726, and in an English Translation by *Thomas Newlin* in 1727. This book contains an interesting enumeration of the numerous conspiracies against the life and throne of Charles the Second during the earlier part of his reign, a panegyric upon Archbishop Sheldon and plentiful abuse of Andrew Marvell. Parker died in unhappy circumstances (see Macaulay's *History*, vol. ii. p. 205), but he left behind him a pious nonjuring son, and his grandson founded the famous publishing firm at Oxford.

[176:1] Grosart, vol. iii. p. 284.

[178:1] Grosart, vol. iii. p. 370.

[178:2] *Ibid.*, p. 382.

CHAPTER VI

LAST YEARS IN THE HOUSE OF COMMONS

MARVELL'S last ten years in the House of Commons were made miserable by the passionate conviction that there existed in high quarters of the State a deep, dangerous, and well-considered plot to subvert the Protestant faith and to destroy by armed force Parliamentary Government in England. Marvell was not the victim of a delusion. Such a plot, plan, or purpose undoubtedly existed, though, as it failed, it is now easy to consider the alarm it created to have been exaggerated.

Marvell was, of all public men then living, the one most deeply imbued with the spirit of our free constitution. Its checks and balances jumped with his humour. His nature was without any taint of fanaticism, nor was he anything of the doctrinaire. He was neither a Richard Baxter nor a John Locke. He had none of the pure Erastianism of Selden, who tells us in his inimitable, cold-blooded way that "a King is a King men have made for their own sakes, for quietness' sake." "Just as in a family one man is appointed to buy the meat," and that "there is no such thing as spiritual jurisdiction; all is civil, the Church's is the same with the Lord Mayor's. The Pope he challenges jurisdiction over all; the Bishops they pretend to it as well as he; the Presbyterians they would have it to themselves, but over whom is all this, the poor layman" (see Selden's *Table Talk*).

This may be excellent good sense but it does not represent Marvell's way of looking at things. He thought more nobly of both church and king.

In Marvell's last book, his famous pamphlet "*An Account of the Growth of Popery and Arbitrary Government in England," printed at Amsterdam and recommended to the reading of all English Protestants*, 1678, which made a prodigious stir and (it is sad to think) paved the way for the "Popish Plot," Marvell sets forth his view of our constitution in language as lofty as it is precise. I know no passage in any of our institutional writers of equal merit.

"For if first we consider the State, the kings of England rule not upon the same terms with those of our neighbour nations, who, having by force or by address usurped that due share which their people had in the government, are now for some ages in the possession of an arbitrary power (which yet no prescription can make legal) and exercise it over their persons and estates in a most tyrannical manner. But here the subjects retain their proportion in the Legislature; the very meanest commoner of England is represented in Parliament, and is a party to those laws by which the Prince is sworn to govern himself and his people. No money is to be levied but by the common consent. No man is for life, limb, goods, or liberty, at the Sovereign's discretion: but we have the same right (modestly understood) in our propriety that the prince hath in his regality: and in all cases where the King is concerned, we have our just remedy as against any private person of the neighbourhood, in the Courts of Westminster Hall or in the High Court of Parliament. His very Prerogative is no more than what the Law has determined. His Broad Seal, which is the legitimate stamp of his pleasure, yet is no longer currant, than upon the trial it is found to be legal. He cannot commit any person by his particular warrant. He cannot himself be witness in any cause: the balance of publick justice being so delicate, that not the hand only but even the breath of the Prince would turn the scale. Nothing is left to the King's will, but all is subjected to his authority: by which means it follows that he can do no wrong, nor can he receive wrong; and a King of England keeping to these measures, may without arrogance, be said to remain the onely intelligent Ruler over a rational People. In recompense therefore and acknowledgment of so good a Government under his influence, his person is most sacred and inviolable; and whatsoever excesses are committed against so high a trust, nothing of them is imputed to him, as being free from the necessity or temptation; but his ministers only are accountable for all, and must answer it at their perils. He hath a vast revenue constantly arising from the hearth of the Householder, the sweat of the Labourer, the rent of the Farmer, the industry of the Merchant, and consequently out of the estate of the Gentleman: a large competence to defray the ordinary expense of the Crown, and maintain its lustre. And if any extraordinary occasion happen, or be but with any probable decency pretended, the whole Land at whatsoever season of the year does yield him a plentiful harvest. So forward are his people's affections to give even to superfluity, that a forainer (or Englishman that hath been long abroad) would think they could neither will nor chuse, but that the asking of a supply were a meer formality, it is so readily granted. He is the fountain of all honours, and has moreover the distribution of so many profitable offices of the Household, of the Revenue, of State, of Law, of Religion, of the Navy and (since his present Majestie's time) of the Army, that it seems as if the Nation could scarce furnish honest men enow to supply all those imployments. So that the Kings of England are in nothing inferiour to other Princes, save in being more abridged from injuring their own subjects: but have as large a field as any of external felicity, wherein to exercise their own virtue, and so reward and incourage it in others. In short, there is nothing that comes nearer in Government to the Divine Perfection, than where the Monarch, as with us, injoys a capacity of doing all the good imaginable to mankind, under a disability to all that is evil."[1]

This was the constitution which Marvell, whose means of information were great and whose curiosity was insatiable, believed to be in danger. No wonder he was agitated.

The politics in which Marvell was immersed during his last years are difficult to unravel and still more difficult to illuminate, for they had their dim origin in the secret thoughts and wavering purposes of the king.

Charles the Second, like many another Englishman guiltless of Stuart blood in his veins, was mainly governed by his dislikes, his pleasures, and his financial necessities. To suppose, as some hasty moralisers have done, that Charles cared for nothing but his women is to misread his character. He had many qualifications to be the chief magistrate of a nation of shopkeepers. He was ever alive to the supreme importance of English trade upon the high seas. His thoughts were often turned in the direction of the Indies, east and west. He took a constant, though not always an honest, interest in the navy. He hated Holland for more reasons than one, but among these reasons was his hatred of England's most formidable and malicious trade competitor. He also disliked her arid and ugly Protestantism, and blood being thicker than water, he hated Holland for what he considered her shabby treatment of his youthful nephew, whose ultimate destiny was happily hidden from Whitehall. Among Charles's many dislikes must be included the Anglican bishops, who had prevented him from keeping his word, and foiled his purpose of a wide toleration. He envied his brother of France the wide culture, the literature and art of Catholicism. He regretted the Reformation, and would have been best pleased to see the English Church in communion with Rome and in possession of "Anglican liberties" akin to those enjoyed by the Gallican Church. Charles was also jealous of Louis the Fourteenth, and in many moods had no mind to play perpetually a second fiddle. He longed for a navy to sweep the seas, for an army strong enough to keep his Parliament in check, and for liberty for himself and for all those of his subjects who were so minded, to hear Mass on Sundays. Behind, and above, and always surrounding these desires and dislikes, was an ever-present, ever-pressing need for money. Like a royal Becky Sharp, Charles might have found it easy to be a patriotic king on five millions a year.

The king was his own Foreign Minister, and being what he was, and swayed by the considerations I have imperfectly described, his foreign policy was necessarily tortuous and perplexing. As Ranke says, "Charles was capable of proposing offensive alliances to the three neighbouring powers, to the Dutch against France, to the French against Spain and Holland, to the Spaniards against France to the detriment of Holland, but in these propositions two fundamental views always recur—demands for money, and assurance of world-wide commerce for England."[1]

Charles first allowed Sir William Temple, a cool, prudent man, to form, in a famous five days' negotiation, the defensive treaty with Holland, which, after Sweden had joined it, became known as the Triple Alliance (1668). This alliance had for its objects mutual promises between the contracting parties to come to each other's assistance by sea and land if attacked by any power (France being here intended), to force Spain to make peace with France on the terms already offered, and to compel France to keep those terms when agreed to by Spain.

The Triple Alliance was not only very popular in England, but was good diplomacy, for it was quite within the range of practical politics that France and Holland might have combined against England; nor could it easily be maintained that the alliance was hostile to France, as it provided that Spain should be forced to accept the terms France had already proposed.

What wrecked the Triple Alliance and prepared the way for the secret Treaty of Dover (1670), was the impossibility of settling those religious difficulties which, despite the Act of Uniformity, were more rampant than ever. The king wanted to patch up peace, and to secure some working plan of comprehension or composure, under cover of which the Catholic religion should be tolerated and Presbyterianism formally recognised. But, king though he was, he could not get his way. The Church and the House of Commons, full as the latter was of his pimps and pensioners, were as obstinate as mules in this matter of toleration. They would neither favour Papists nor Dissenters, protested against Indulgences as unconstitutional, and clamoured for a rigorous administration of that penal legislation against Nonconformists which they had purchased with so many and such lavish supplies. As a matter of fact, these penal laws were very fitfully enforced. In London they were often totally disregarded, and we read of congregations numbering two thousand openly attending Presbyterian services. The Lord Mayor for the time being took his orders direct from the king.

What was Charles to do? After the fall of Clarendon, the king's favourite privy councillors, called the "Cabal," because the initial letters of their names formed a word which for some time previously had been in common use, represent only too faithfully the confusion and corruption of the times. Clifford was a zealous Roman, Arlington a cautious one, Buckingham a free-thinker and mocker, friendly to France and on good terms with the more advanced English sectaries; Ashley made no pretence to be a Christian, but favoured philosophic toleration; whilst Lauderdale, one of the most learned ministers that ever sat in council (so Ranke says[1]), was, as a matter of profession, a Presbyterian, but in reality a man wholly and slavishly devoted to the king's interests, and prepared at any moment to pour into the kingdom soldiers from Scotland to purge or suppress all Free Institutions.

Irritated, disgusted, thwarted, and annoyed, the king, acting, it well may be, under the influence of his accomplished sister, the beautiful and ill-fated Duchess of Orleans, struck up, to use Marvell's own words, "an invisible league with France." The negotiations were either by word of mouth or by letters which have been burnt. Dr. Lingard in his history gives an interesting account of this mysterious transaction. Two things are apparent as the objects of the Treaty of Dover. The Dutch Republic is to be destroyed, and the cause of Catholicism in England is to be promoted and maintained. It was this latter object that seems most to have excited the hopes of the Duchess of Orleans. A woman's hand is traceable throughout. Charles promised to profess himself openly a Roman Catholic at the time that should appear to be most expedient, and subsequently to that profession he was to join with Louis in making war upon the Dutch Republic. At the date of this bewildering agreement, it was high treason by statute even to *say* that Charles was a Roman Catholic. In case the king's public conversion should lead to disturbances, Louis promised an "aid" of two millions of *livres* and an armed force of six thousand men. He also agreed to pay the whole cost of the Dutch War *on land*, and to contribute thirty men-of-war to the English fleet. Holland once crushed, England's share of the plunder was to be Walcheren, Sluys, and Cadsand. A remarkable conversion! It is difficult to suppose that either Charles or Louis were quite serious over this part of the business. Yet there it is. The Catholic provisions of the secret Treaty of Dover were only known to Clifford, whose soul was fired by them, and to Arlington, who did not share the confident hopes of his co-religionist. Clifford thought there were thousands of Englishmen "of light and leading" among the English Catholics who would be both willing and able to assume the burdens of the State and to rally round a Catholic king. Arlington thought otherwise.

The king's public conversion never took place. No hint was given of any such impending event. Parliament met on the 24th of October 1670, and after hearing a good deal about the Triple Alliance and voting large sums of money, was prorogued in April 1671, and did not meet again till February 1673.

To pick a quarrel with the Dutch was never difficult. Marvell tells us how it was done. "A sorry yacht, but bearing the English Jack, in August 1671 sails into the midst of the Dutch fleet, singles out the Admiral, shooting twice as they call it, sharp upon him. Which must sure have appeared as ridiculous and unnatural as for a lark to dare the hobby." The Dutch admiral asking "Why," was told "because he and his whole fleet had failed to strike sail to his small craft." The Dutch commander then "civilly excused it as a matter of the first instance, and in which he could have no instruction, therefore proper to be referred to their masters, and so they parted. The yacht having thus acquitted itself, returned fraught with the quarrel she was sent for."[1] Surinam was a perpetual *casus belli*. Some offence against the law of nations was always happening there. A third matter, very full of gunpowder, was made great use of by the promoters of the war already agreed upon. A picture had been hung at Dort representing De Witt sailing up the Medway very much in the manner described in Marvell's poem. Medals also had been struck and distributed in commemoration of the same event. War was declared against Holland by England and France in March 1672. The Declaration of War was preceded by the Declaration of Indulgence, whereby, wrote Marvell, "all the penal laws against Papists for which former Parliaments had given so many supplies, and against Nonconformists for which this Parliament had paid more largely, were at one instant suspended in order to defraud the nation of all that religion which they had so dearly purchased, and for which they ought at least, the bargain being broke, to have been reimbursed."[2]

The unconstitutional suspension of bad laws put lovers of freedom in a predicament. Marvell was what he calls a "composure," that is a "comprehension," man. In the *Growth of Popery* he sorrowfully admits that it is the gravest reproach of human wisdom that no man seems able or willing to find out the due temper of Government in divine matters.

"Insomuch that it is no great adventure to say, that the world was better ordered under the ancient monarchies and commonwealths, that the number of virtuous men was then greater, and that the Christians found fairer quarter under those than among themselves, nor hath there any advantage accrued unto mankind from that most perfect and practical model of humane society, except the speculation of a better way to future happiness, concerning which the very guides disagree, and of those few that follow, it will suffer no man to pass without paying at their turnpikes." (Vol. iv. p. 280.)

The French Alliance made the war, though with Holland, unpopular. Writers had to be hired to defend it. France was supposed to look on with much composure as her two maritime competitors battered each other's fleets. At sea the honours were divided between the Dutch and the English. On land Louis had it all his own way. Besides, rumours got abroad of an uncomfortable plot to restore Popery. Jesuits seemed to abound. Roman Catholics asserted themselves, the laws being suspended. An army was collected at Blackheath. The Treasury was closed. Charles had been badly bled by the goldsmiths or bankers, who had charged him £12 per cent.; but in commercial centres Acts of Bankruptcy are seldom popular, and though the bankers were compelled to be content with £6 per cent., the closing of the Treasury brought ruin into many homes.

When Parliament met in February 1673, its temper was bad. It would have nothing to do with the Declaration of Indulgence, and though the king had told them, in the round set terms he could so well command, that he was resolved to stick to his declaration, he had to give way and to see the House busy itself with a Test Bill that drove all Roman Catholics, from the Duke of York (who had "gone over" in the spring of 1672) downwards, out of office.

The only effect of Charles's policy was to mitigate the hostility of the House of Commons to Protestant Dissenters, and to drive it to concentrate its jealousy upon the Catholics. Any lurking idea of the king declaring himself a Romanist had to be abandoned. His hatred of Parliament increased. He lost all sense of shame, and frankly became a pensioner of France. In 1676 he concluded a second secret treaty, whereby both Louis and himself bound themselves to enter into no engagements with other powers without consent, and in case of rebellion within their realms to come to each other's assistance. Louis agreed to make Charles an annual allowance of a hundred thousand, afterwards increased to two hundred thousand *livres*. This money was largely spent in bribing the House of Commons. The French ambassador was allowed an extra grant of a thousand crowns a month to keep a table for hungry legislators.[1] Did not Marvell do well to be angry?

Some of Marvell's letters belonging to this gloomy period are full of interest.

To William Ramsden, Esq.

"Nov. 28, 1670.

"DEAR WILL,—I need not tell you I am always thinking of you. All that has happened, which is remarkable, since I wrote, is as follows: The Lieutenancy of London, chiefly Sterlin the Mayor, and Sir J. Robinson, alarmed the King continually with the Conventicles there. So the King sent them strict and large powers. The Duke of York every Sunday would come over thence to look to the peace. To say truth, they met in numerous open assemblys, without any dread of government. But the train bands in the city, and soldiery in Southwark and suburbs, harassed and abused them continually; they wounded many, and killed some Quakers especially, while they took all patiently. Hence arose two things of great remark. The Lieutenancy, having got orders to their mind, pick out Hays and Jekill, the innocentist of the whole party, to show their power on. They offer them illegal bonds of five thousand pounds a man, which if they would not enter into, they must go to prison. So they were committed, and at last (but it is a very long story) got free. Some friends engaged for them. The other was the tryal of Pen and Mead, quakers, at the Old Baily. The jury not finding them guilty, as the Recorder and Mayor would have had them, they were kept without meat or drink some three days, till almost starved, but would not alter their verdict; so fined and imprisoned. There is a book out which relates all the passages, which were very pertinent, of the prisoners, but prodigiously barbarous by the Mayor and Recorder. The Recorder, among the rest, commended the Spanish Inquisition, saying it would never be well till we had something like it. The King had occasion for sixty thousand pounds. Sent to borrow it of the city. Sterlin, Robinson, and all the rest of that faction, were at it many a week, and could not get above ten thousand. The fanatics under persecution, served his Majesty. The other party, both in court and city, would have prevented it. But the King protested mony would be acceptable. So the King patched up, out of the Chamber, and other ways, twenty thousand pounds. The fanatics, of all sorts, forty thousand. The King, though against many of his council, would have the Parliament sit this twenty-fourth of October. He, and the Keeper spoke of nothing but to have money. Some one million three hundred thousand pounds, to pay off the debts at interest; and eight hundred thousand for a brave navy next Spring. Both speeches forbid to be printed, for the King said very little, and the Keeper, it was thought, too much in his politic simple discourse of foreign affairs. The House was thin and obsequious. They voted at first they would supply him according to his occasions, *Nemine*, as it was remarked, *contradicente*; but few affirmatives, rather a silence as of men ashamed and unwilling. Sir R. Howard, Seymour, Temple, Car, and Hollis, openly took leave of their former party, and fell to head the King's busyness. There is like to be a terrible Act of Conventicles. The Prince of Orange here is much made of. The King owes him a great deal of mony. The Paper is full.—I am yours," etc.

The trial of William Penn and William Mead at the Old Bailey for a tumultuous assembly, written by themselves, may be read in the *State Trials*, vol. vi. The trial was the occasion of Penn's famous remark to the Recorder of London, who, driven wellnigh distracted by Penn's dialectics, exclaimed, "If I should suffer you to ask questions till to-morrow morning you would never be the wiser." "That," replied Penn, "would be according as the answers are."

To William Ramsden, Esq.

(Undated.)

"DEAR WILL,—The Parliament are still proceeding, but not much advanced on their eight hundred thousand pounds Bill on money at interest, offices, and lands; and the Excise Bills valued at four hundred thousand pounds a year. The first for the navy, which scarce will be set out. The last to be for paying one million three hundred thousand pounds, which the King owes at interest, and perhaps may be given for four, five, or six years, as the House chances to be in humour. But an accident happened which liked to have spoiled all: Sir John Coventry having moved for an imposition on the playhouses, Sir John Berkenhead, to excuse them, sayed they had been of great service to the King. Upon which Sir John Coventry desired that gentleman to explain whether he meant the men or the women players. Hereupon it is imagined, that, the House adjourning from Tuesday before till Thursday after Christmas-day, on the very Tuesday night of the adjournment, twenty-five of the Duke of Monmouth's troop, and some few foot, layed in wait from ten at night till two in the morning, by Suffolk-street, and as he returned from the Cock, where he supped, to his own house, they threw him down, and with a knife cut off almost the end of his nose; but company coming made them fearful to finish it, so they marched off. Sir Thomas Sands, lieutenant of the troop, commanded the party; and O'Brian, the Earl of Inchequin's son, was a principal actor. The Court hereupon sometimes thought to carry it with a high hand, and question Sir John for his words, and maintain the action. Sometimes they flagged in their counsels. However, the King commanded Sir Thomas Clarges, and Sir W. Pultney, to release Wroth and Lake, who were two of the actors, and taken. But the night before the House met they surrendered them again. The House being but sullen the next day, the Court did not oppose adjourning for some days longer till it was filled. Then the House went upon Coventry's busyness, and voted that they would go upon nothing else whatever till they had passed a Bill, as they did, for Sands, O'Brian, Parry, and Reeves, to come in by the sixteenth of February, or else be condemned, and never to be pardoned, but by an express Act of Parliament, and their names therein inserted, for fear of being pardoned in some general act of grace. Farther of all such actions, for the future on any man, felony, without clergy; and who shall otherwise strike or wound any parliament-man, during his attendance, or going or coming, imprisonment for a year, treble damages, and incapacity. This Bill having in some few days been dispatched to the Lords, the House has since gone on in grand Committee upon the first eight hundred thousand pounds Bill, but are not yet half way. But now the Lords, instead of the sixteenth of February, put twenty-five days after the King's royal assent, and that registered in their journal; they disagree in several other things, but adhere in that first, which is most material. Adhere, in this place, signifies not to be retracted, and excludes a free conference. So that this week the Houses will be in danger of splitting, without much wisdom or force. For considering that Sir Thomas Sands was the very person sent to Clarges and Pultney, that O'Brian was concealed in the Duke of Monmouth's lodgings, that Wroth and Lake were bayled at the sessions by order from Mr. Attorney, and that all persons and things are perfectly discovered, that act will not be passed without great consequence. George's father obliges you much in Tangier. Prince Edgar is dying. The Court is at the highest pitch of want and luxury, and the people full of discontent, Remember me to yourselves."

To William Ramsden, Esq.

(Undated.)

"DEAR WILL,—I think I have not told you that, on our Bill of Subsidy, the Lord Lucas made a fervent bold speech against our prodigality in giving, and the weak looseness of the government, the King being present; and the Lord Clare another to persuade the King that he ought not to be present. But all this had little encouragement, not being seconded. Copys going about everywhere, one of them was brought into the Lords' House, and Lord Lucas was asked whether it was his. He sayd part was, and part was not. Thereupon they took advantage, and sayed it was a libel even against Lucas himself. On this they voted it a libel, and to be burned by the hangman. Which was done; but the sport was, the hangman burned the Lords' order with it. I take the last quarrel betwixt us and the Lords to be as the ashes of that speech. Doubtless you have heard, before this time, how Monmouth, Albemarle, Dunbane, and seven or eight gentlemen, fought with the watch, and killed a poor bedle. They have all got their pardons, for Monmouth's sake; but it is an act of great scandal. The King of France is at Dunkirke. We have no fleet out, though we gave the Subsidy Bill, valued at eight hundred thousand pounds, for that purpose. I believe, indeed, he will attempt nothing on us, but leave us to dy a natural death. For indeed never had poor nation so many complicated, mortal, incurable, diseases. You know the Dutchess of York is dead. All gave her for a Papist. I think it will be my lot to go on an honest fair employment into Ireland. Some have smelt the court of Rome at that distance. There I hope I shall be out of the smell of our.... —Yours," etc.

To a Friend in Persia.

"*August 9, 1671.*

"DEAR SIR,—I have yours of the 12th of October 1670, which was in all respects most welcome to me, except when I considered that to write it you endured some pain, for you say your hand is not yet recovered. If I could say any thing to you towards the advancement of your affairs, I could, with a better conscience, admit you should spend so much of your precious time, as you do, upon me. But you know how far those things are out of my road, tho', otherwise, most desirous in all things to be serviceable to you. God's good providence, which hath through so dangerous a disease and so many difficultys preserved and restored you, will, I doubt not, conduct you to a prosperous issue, and the perfection of your so laudable undertakings. And, under that, your own good genius, in conjunction with your brother here, will, I hope, though at the distance of England and Persia, in good time operate extraordinary effects; for the magnetism of two souls, rightly touched, works beyond all natural limits, and it would be indeed too unequal, if good nature should not have at least as large a sphere of activity, as malice, envy, and detraction, which are, it seems, part of the returns from Gombroon and Surat. All I can say to you in that matter is, that you must, seeing it will not be better, stand upon your guard; for in this world a good cause signifys little, unless it be as well defended. A man may starve at the feast of good conscience. My fencing master in Spain, after he had instructed me all he could, told me, I remember, there was yet one secret, against which there was no defence, and that was, to give the first blow. I know your maxim, *Qui festinat ditescere, non erit innocens*. Indeed while you preserve that mind, you will have the blessing both of God and man. In general I perceive, and am very glad of it, that by your good management, your friends here get ground, and the flint in your adversarys' hearts begins to be mollifyed. Now after my usual method, leaving to others what relates to busyness, I address myself, which is all I am good for, to be your gazettier. I am sorry to perceive that mine by the Armenian miscarryed. Tho' there was nothing material in it, the thoughts of friends are too valuable to fall into the hands of a stranger. I wrote the last February at large, and wish it a better passage. In this perhaps I may interfere something with that, chusing rather to repeat than omit. The King having, upon pretence of the great preparations of his neighbours, demanded three hundred thousand pounds for his navy (though in conclusion he hath not set out any) and that the Parliament should pay his debts, which the ministers would never particularize to the House of Commons, our House gave several bills. You see how far things were stretched, though beyond reason, there being no satisfaction how those debts were contracted, and all men foreseeing that what was given would not be applyed to discharge the debts, which I hear are at this day risen to four millions, but diverted as formerly. Nevertheless such was the number of the constant courtiers increased by the apostate patriots, who were bought off, for that turn, some at six, others ten, one at fifteen thousand pounds in money, besides what offices, lands, and reversions, to others, that it is a mercy they gave not away the whole land, and liberty, of England. The Earl of Clare made a very bold and rational harangue, the King being present, against the King's sitting among the Lords, contrary to former precedents, during their debates; but he was not seconded. The King had this April prorogued, upon the Houses cavilling, and their harsh conferences concerning some bills, the Parliament from this April till the 16th of April 1672. Sir John Coventry's Bill against Cutting Noses passed, and O'Brian and Sir Thomas Sands, not appearing at the Old Baily by the time limited, stand attainted and outlawed, without possibility of pardon. The Duke of Buckingham is again one hundred and forty thousand pounds in debt, and, by this prorogation, his creditors have time to tear all his lands in pieces. The House of Commons has run almost to the end of their line, and are grown extreme chargeable to the King, and odious to the people. Lord St. John, Marquess of Westminster's son, one of the House of Commons, Sir Robert Howard, Sir John Benet, Lord Arlington's brother, Sir William Bucknoll, the brewer, all of the House, in fellowship with some others of the city, have farmed the old customs, with the new act of Imposition upon Wines, and the Wine Licenses, at six hundred thousand pounds a year, to begin this Michaelmas. You may be sure they have covenants not to be losers. They have signed and sealed ten thousand pounds a year more to the Duchess of Cleveland, who has likewise near ten thousand pounds a year out of the new farm of the country excise of Beer and Ale, five thousand pounds a year out of the Post Office, and, they say, the reversion of all the King's leases, the reversion of places all in the Custom House, the green wax, and indeed, what not? All promotions, spiritual and temporal, pass under her cognizance. Buckingham runs out of all with the Lady Shrewsbury, by whom he believes he had a son, to whom the King stood godfather; it dyed, young Earl of Coventry, and was buryed in the sepulchre of his fathers. The King of France made a warlike progresse this summer through his conquests of Flanders, but kept the peace there, and detains still the Dutchy of Lorain, and has stired up the German Princes against the free towns. The Duke of Brunswick has taken the town of Brunswick; and now the Bishop of Cullen is attacking the city of Colen. We truckle to France in all things, to the prejudice of our honour. Barclay is still Lieutenant of Ireland; but he was forced to come over to pay ten thousand pounds rent to his Landlady Cleveland. My Lord Angier, who bought of Sir George Carteret for eleven thousand pounds, the Vice-treasurership of Ireland, worth five thousand pounds a year, is, betwixt knavery and foolery, turned out. Dutchess of York and Prince Edgar, dead. None left but daughters. One Blud, outlawed for a plot to take Dublin Castle, and who seized on the Duke of Ormond here last year, and might have killed him, a most bold, and yet sober fellow, some months ago seized the crown and sceptre in the Tower, took them away, and if he had killed the keeper, might have carried them clear off. He, being taken, astonished the King and Court, with the generosity, and wisdom, of his answers. He, and all his accomplices, for his sake, are discharged by the King, to the wonder of all.—Yours," etc.

To William Ramsden, Esq.

"*June 1672.*

"DEAR WILL,—Affairs begin to alter, and men talk of a peace with Holland, and taking them into our protection; and it is my opinion it will be before Michaelmas, for some reasons, not fit to write. We cannot have a peace with France and Holland both. The Dutch are now brought very low; but Amsterdam, and some other provinces, are resolved to stand out till the last. De-wit is stabbed, and dead of his wounds. It was at twelve a clock at night, the 11th of this month, as he came from the council at the Hague. Four men wounded him with their swords. But his own letter next morning to the States says nothing appeared mortal. The whole Province of Utrecht is yielding up. No man can conceive the condition of the State of Holland, in this juncture, unless he can at the same time conceive an earthquake, an hurricane, and the deluge. France is potent and subtle. Here have been several fires of late. One at St. Catherine's, which burned about six score or two hundred houses, and some seven or eight ships. Another in Bishopsgate-street. Another in Crichet Fryars. Another in Southwark; and some elsewhere. You may be sure all the old talk is hereupon revived. There was the other day, though not on this occasion, a severe proclamation issued out against all who shall vent false news, or discourse ill concerning affairs of state. So that in writing to you I run the risque of making a breech in the commandment.—Yours," etc.

The following letter deals with another matter of human concern than politics, for it seeks to condole with a father who has lost an only son.

To Sir John Trott

(Undated.)

"HONOURED SIR,—I have not that vanity to believe, if you weigh your late loss by the common ballance, that any thing I can write to you should lighten your resentments: nor if you measure things by the rules of christianity, do I think it needful to comfort you in your duty and your son's happyness. Only having a great esteem and affection for you, and the grateful memory of him that is departed being still green and fresh upon my spirit, I cannot forbear to inquire, how you have stood the second shock at your sad meeting of friends in the country. I know that the very sight of those who have been witnesses of our better fortune, doth but serve to reinforce a calamity. I know the contagion of grief and infection of tears, and especially when it runs in a blood. And I myself could sooner imitate than blame those innocent relentings of nature, so that they spring from tenderness only and humanity, not from an implacable sorrow. The tears of a family may flow together like those little drops that compact the rainbow, and if they be placed with the same advantage towards Heaven as those are to the sun, they too have their splendour; and like that bow, while they unbend into seasonable showers, yet they promise, that there shall not be a second flood. But the dissoluteness of grief, the prodigality of sorrow, is neither to be indulged in a man's self, nor complied with in others. If that were allowable in these cases, Eli's was the readyest way and highest compliment of mourning, who fell back from his seat and broke his neck. But neither does that precedent hold. For though he had been Chancellor, and in effect King of Israel, for so many years (and such men value, as themselves, their losses at an higher rate than others), yet, when he heard that Israel was overcome, that his two sons Hophni and Phineas were slain in one day, and saw himself so without hope of issue, and which imbittered it farther, without succession to the government, yet he fell not till the news that the ark of God was taken. I pray God that we may never have the same parallel perfected in our publick concernments. Then we shall need all the strength of grace and nature to support us. But on a private loss, and sweetened with so many circumstances as yours, to be impatient, to be uncomfortable would be to dispute with God. Though an only son be inestimable, yet it is like Jonah's sin, to be angry at God for the withering of his shadow. Zipporah, though the delay had almost cost her husband his life, yet, when he did but circumcise her son, in a womanish peevishness reproached Moses as a bloody husband. But if God take the son himself, but spare the father, shall we say that He is a bloody God? He that gave His own son, may He not take ours? It is pride that makes a rebel; and nothing but the over-weening of ourselves and our own things that raises us against Divine Providence. Whereas Abraham's obedience was better than sacrifice. And if God please to accept both, it is indeed a farther tryal, but a greater honour. I could say over upon this beaten occasion most of those lessons of morality and religion which have been so often repeated, and are as soon forgotten. We abound with precept, but we want examples. You, sir, that have all these things in your memory, and the clearness of whose judgment is not to be obscured by any greater interposition, should be exemplary to others in your own practice. 'Tis true, it is an hard task to learn and teach at the same time. And, where yourselves are the experiment, it is as if a man should dissect his own body, and read the anatomy lecture. But I will not heighten the difficulty while I advise the attempt. Only, as in difficult things, you would do well to make use of all that may strengthen and assist you; the word of God; the society of good men; and the books of the ancients; there is one way more, which is by diversion, business, and activity; which are also necessary to be used in their season. But I myself, who live to so little purpose, can have little authority or ability to advise you in it, who are a person that are and may be much more so, generally useful. All that I have been able to do since, hath been to write this sorry Elogy of your son, which if it be as good as I could wish, it is as yet no indecent employment. However, I know you will take any thing kindly from your very affectionate friend, and most humble servant."

Milton died on the 8th of November 1674. Marvell remained among the poet's intimate friends until the end, and intended to write his life. It is idle to mourn the loss of an unwritten book, but Marvell's life of Milton would have been a treasure.[1]

When Parliament met on the 13th of April 1675, members found in their places a mock-speech from the throne. They *knew* the hand that had penned it. It was a daring production and ran as follows:—

His Majesty's Most Gracious Speech to Both Houses of Parliament.

"MY LORDS AND GENTLEMEN,—I told you at our last meeting, the winter was the fittest time for business, and truly I thought so, till my Lord Treasurer assured me the spring was the best season for sallads and subsidies. I hope therefore that April will not prove so unnatural a month, as not to afford some kind showers on my parched exchequer, which gapes for want of them. Some of you, perhaps, will think it dangerous to make me too rich; but I do not fear it; for I promise you faithfully, whatever you give me I will always want; and although in other things my word may be thought a slender authority, yet in that, you may rely on me, I will never break it.

"MY LORDS AND GENTLEMEN,—I can bear my straits with patience; but my Lord Treasurer does protest to me, that the revenue, as it now stands, will not serve him and me too. One of us must pinch for it, if you do not help me. I must speak freely to you: I am under bad circumstances, for besides my harlots in service, my reformado concubines lye heavy upon me. I have a passable good estate, I confess, but, God's-fish, I have a great charge upon 't. Here's my Lord Treasurer can tell, that all the money designed for next summer's guards must, of necessity, be applyed to the next year's cradles and swadling-cloths. What shall we do for ships then? I hint this only to you, it being your busyness, not mine. I know, by experience, I can live without ships. I lived ten years abroad without, and never had my health better in my life; but how you will be without, I leave to yourselves to judge, and therefore hint this only by the bye: I do not insist upon it. There's another thing I must press more earnestly, and that is this:—It seems a good part of my revenue will expire in two or three years, except you will be pleased to continue it. I have to say for 't, pray, why did you give me so much as you have done, unless you resolve to give on as fast as I call for it? The nation hates you already for giving so much, and I'll hate you too, if you do not give me more. So that if you stick not to me, you must not have a friend in England. On the other hand, if you will give me the revenue I desire, I shall be able to do those things for your religion and liberty, that I have had long in my thoughts, but cannot effect them without a little more money to carry me through. Therefore look to 't and take notice that if you do not make me rich enough to undo you, it shall lie at your doors. For my part I wash my hands on 't. But that I may gain your good opinion, the best way is to acquaint you what I have done to deserve it, out of my royal care for your religion and your property. For the first, my proclamation is a true picture of my mind, He that cannot, as in a glass, see my zeal for the Church of England, does not deserve any farther satisfaction, for I declare him wilful, abominable, and not good. Some may, perhaps, be startled, and cry, how comes this sudden change? To which I answer, I am a changling, and that's sufficient, I think. But to convince men farther, that I mean what I say, there are these arguments:—

"First, I tell you so, and you know I never break my word.

"Secondly, My Lord Treasurer says so, and he never told a lye in his life.

"Thirdly, My Lord Lauderdale will undertake it for me; and I should be loath, by any act of mine, he should forfeit the credit he has with you.

"If you desire more instances of my zeal, I have them for you. For example, I have converted my natural sons from Popery; and I may say, without vanity, it was my own work, so much the more peculiarly mine than the begetting them. 'Twould do one's heart good to hear how prettily George can read already in the Psalter. They are all fine children, God bless 'em, and so like me in their understandings. But, as I was saying, I have, to please you, given a pension to your favourite my Lord Lauderdale; not so much that I thought he wanted it, as that you would take it kindly. I have made Carwell dutchess of Portsmouth, and married her sister to the Earl of Pembroke. I have, at my brother's request, sent my Lord Inchequin into Barbary, to settle the Protestant Religion among the Moors, and an English Interest at Tangier. I have made Crew Bishop of Durham, and, at the first word of my Lady Portsmouth, Prideaux Bishop of Chichester. I know not, for my part, what factious men would have; but this I am sure of, my predecessors never did anything like this, to gain the good will of their subjects. So much for your religion, and now for your property. My behaviour to the Bankers is a publick instance; and the proceedings between Mrs. Hyde and Mrs. Sutton for private ones, are such convincing evidences, that it will be needless to say any more to 't.

"I must now acquaint you, that, by my Lord Treasurer's advice, I have made a considerable retrenchment upon my expenses in candles and charcoal, and do not intend to stop there, but will, with your help, look into the late embezzlements of my dripping-pans and kitchen-stuff; of which, by the way, upon my conscience, neither my Lord Treasurer nor my Lord Lauderdale are guilty. I tell you my opinion; but if you should find them dabling in that busyness, I tell you plainly, I leave 'em to you; for, I would have the world to know, I am not a man to be cheated.

"My Lords and Gentlemen, I desire you to believe me as you have found me; and I do solemnly promise you, that whatsoever you give me shall be specially managed with the same conduct, trust, sincerity, and prudence, that I have ever practised, since my happy restoration."[1]

Mock King's Speeches have often been made, but this is the first, and I think still the best of them all.

There was no shaking off religion from the debates of those days. A new Oaths Bill suddenly appeared in the House of Lords, where it gave rise to one of the greatest debates that assembly has ever witnessed, lasting seventeen days. The bishops were baited by the peers with great spirit, and the report of the proceedings may still be read with gusto.

Marvell, in his *Growth of Popery*, thus describes what happened:—

"While these things were upon the anvil, the 10th of November was come for the Parliament's sitting, but that was put off till the 13th of April 1675.

And in the meantime, which fell out most opportune for the conspirators, these counsels were matured, and something further to be contrived, that was yet wanting; the Parliament accordingly meeting, and the House of Lords, as well as that of the Commons, being in deliberation of several wholesome bills, such as the present state of the nation required, the great design came out in a bill unexpectedly offered one morning in the House of Lords, whereby all such as injoyed any beneficial office, or imployment, ecclesiastical, civil, or military, to which was added privy counsellors, justices of the peace, and members of Parliament, were under a penalty to take the oath, and make the declaration, and abhorrence, insuring:—

'I A. B. do declare, that it is not lawful upon any pretence whatever to take up arms against the King, and that I do abhor that traiterous position of taking arms by his authority against his person, or against those that are commissioned by him in pursuance of such commission. And I do swear, that I will not at any time indeavour the alteration of the government either in Church or State. So help me God.'

"This same oath had been brought into the House of Commons in the plague year at Oxford, to have been imposed upon the nation, but there, by the assistance of those very same persons that now introduce it, 'twas thrown out, for fear of a general infection of the vitals of this kingdom; and though it passed then in a particular bill, known by the name of the Five Mile Act, because it only concerned the non-conformist preachers, yet even in that, it was thoroughly opposed by the late Earl of Southampton, whose judgement might well have been reckoned for the standard of prudence and loyalty."[1]

Of the proposed oath Marvell says, "No Conveyancer could ever in more compendious or binding terms have drawn a dissettlement of the whole birthright of England."

This was no mere legal quibbling.

"These things are no niceties, or remote considerations (though in making of laws, and which must come afterwards under construction of judges, *durante bene placito*, all cases are to be put and imagined) but there being an act in Scotland for 20,000 men to march into England upon call, and so great a body of English soldiery in France, within summons, besides what foreigners may be obliged by treaty to furnish, and it being so fresh in memory, what sort of persons had lately been in commission among us, to which add the many books then printed by license, writ, some by men of the black, one of the green cloth, wherein the absoluteness of the English monarchy is against all law asserted.

"All these considerations put together were sufficient to make any honest and well advised man to conceive indeed, that upon the passing of this oath and declaration, the whole sum of affairs depended.

"It grew therefore to the greatest contest, that has perhaps ever been in Parliament, wherein those Lords, that were against this oath, being assured of their own loyalty and merit, stood up now for the English liberties with the same genius, virtue, and courage, that their noble ancestors had formerly defended the great Charter of England, but with so much greater commendation, in that they had here a fairer field and a more civil way of decision; they fought it out under all the disadvantages imaginable; they were overlaid by numbers; the noise of the House, like the wind, was against them, and if not the sun, the fireside was always in their faces; nor being so few, could they, as their adversaries, withdraw to refresh themselves in a whole day's ingagement: yet never was there a clearer demonstration how dull a thing is humane eloquence, and greatness how little, when the bright truth discovers all things in their proper colours and dimensions, and shining, shoots its beams thorow all their fallacies. It might be injurious, where all of them did so excellently well, to attribute more to any one of those Lords than another, unless because the Duke of Buckingham and the Earl of Shaftesbury, have been the more reproached for this brave action, it be requisite by a double proportion of praise to set them two on equal terms with the rest of their companions in honour. The particular relation in this debate, which lasted many days, with great eagerness on both sides, and the reasons but on one, was in the next Session burnt by order of the Lords, but the sparks of it will eternally fly in their adversaries' faces."[1]

In a letter to his constituents, dated April 22, 1675, Marvell was content to say: "The Lords sate the whole day yesterday till ten at night without rising (and the King all the while but of our addresses present) upon their Bill of Test in both houses and are not yet come to the question of committing it."

After prolonged discussion the Oath Bill was sent to the Commons, where doubtless it must have passed, had not a furious privilege quarrel over Sir John Fagg's case made prorogation in June almost a necessity. In October Parliament met again, and at once resolved itself into a Committee upon Religion to prevent the growth of Popery. This time the king made almost an end of the Parliament by a prorogation which lasted from November 1675 until February 1677—a period of fifteen months.

On the re-assembling of Parliament the Duke of Buckingham fathered the argument much used during the long recess, that a prorogation extending beyond twelve months was in construction of law a dissolution.

For the expression of this opinion and the refusal to recant it the Duke of Buckingham and three other lords were ordered to the Tower, the king being greatly angered by the duke's request that his cook might be allowed to wait on him. On this incident Marvell remarks: "Thus a prorogation without precedent was to be warranted by an imprisonment without example. A sad instance! Whereby the dignity of Parliament and especially of the House of Peers did at present much suffer and may probably more for the future, *for nothing but Parliament can destroy Parliament*. If a House shall once be felon of itself and stop its own breath, taking away that liberty of speech which the King verbally, and of course, allows them (as now they had done in both houses) to what purpose is it coming thither?"[1]

The character of this House of Commons did not improve with age.

Marvell writes in the *Growth of Popery*:—

"In matters of money they seem at first difficult, but having been discoursed with in private, they are set right, and begin to understand it better themselves, and to convert their brethren: for they are all of them to be bought and sold, only their number makes them cheaper, and each of them doth so overvalue himself, that sometimes they outstand or let slip their own market.

"It is not to be imagined, how small things, in this case, even members of great estates will stoop at, and most of them will do as much for hopes as others for fruition, but if their patience be tired out, they grow at last mutinous, and revolt to the country, till some better occasion offer.

"Among these are some men of the best understanding were they of equal integrity, who affect to ingross all business, to be able to quash any good motion by parliamentary skill, unless themselves be the authors, and to be the leading men of the House, and for their natural lives to continue so. But these are men that have been once fooled, most of them, and discovered, and slighted at Court, so that till some turn of State shall let them in their adversaries' place, in the mean time they look sullen, make big motions, and contrive specious bills for the subject, yet only wait the opportunity to be the instruments of the same counsels which they oppose in others.

"There is a third part still remaining, but as contrary in themselves as light and darkness; those are either the worst, or the best of men; the first are most profligate persons, they have neither estates, consciences, nor good manners, yet are therefore picked out as the necessary men, and whose votes will go furthest; the charges of their elections are defrayed, whatever they amount to, tables are kept for them at Whitehall, and through Westminster, that they may be ready at hand, within call of a question: all of them are received into pension, and know their pay-day, which they never fail of: insomuch that a great officer was pleased to say, 'That they came about him like so many jack-daws for cheese at the end of every Session.' If they be not in Parliament, they must be in prison, and as they are protected themselves, by privilege, so they sell their protections to others, to the obstruction so many years together of the law of the land, and the publick justice; for these it is, that the long and frequent adjournments are calculated, but all whether the court, or the monopolizers of the country party, or those that profane the title of old cavaliers, do equally, though upon differing reasons, like death apprehend a dissolution. But notwithstanding these, there is an handful of salt, a sparkle of soul, that hath hitherto preserved this gross body from putrefaction, some gentlemen that are constant, invariable, indeed Englishmen; such as are above hopes, or fears, or dissimulation, that can neither flatter, nor betray their king or country: but being conscious of their own loyalty and integrity, proceed throw good and bad report, to acquit themselves in their duty to God, their prince, and their nation; although so small a scantling in number, that men can scarce reckon of them more than a *quorum*; insomuch that it is less difficult to conceive how fire was first brought to light in the world than how any good thing could ever be produced out of an House of Commons so constituted, unless as that is imagined to have come from the rushing of trees, or battering of rocks together, by accident, so these, by their clashing with one another, have struck out an useful effect from so unlikely causes. But whatsoever casual good hath been wrought at any time by the assimilation of ambitious, factious and disappointed members, to the little, but solid, and unbiassed party, the more frequent ill effects, and consequences of so unequal a mixture, so long continued, are demonstrable and apparent. For while scarce any man comes thither with respect to the publick service, but in design to make and raise his fortune, it is not to be expressed, the debauchery, and lewdness, which, upon occasion of election to Parliaments, are now grown habitual thorow the nation. So that the vice, and the expence, are risen to such a prodigious height, that few sober men can indure to stand to be chosen on such conditions. From whence also arise feuds, and perpetual animosities, over most of the counties and corporations, while gentlemen of worth, spirit, and ancient estates and dependances, see themselves overpowered in their own neighbourhood by the drunkness and bribery, of their competitors. But if nevertheless any worthy person chance to carry the election, some mercenary or corrupt sheriff makes a double return, and so the cause is handed to the Committee of elections, who ask no better, but are ready to adopt his adversary into the House if he be not legitimate. And if the gentleman agrieved seek his remedy against the sheriff in Westminster-Hall, and the proofs be so palpable, that the King's Bench cannot invent how to do him injustice, yet the major part of the twelve judges shall upon better consideration vacate the sheriff's fine and reverse the judgement; but those of them that dare dissent from their brethren are in danger to be turned off the bench without any cause assigned. While men therefore care not thus how they get into the House of Commons, neither can it be expected that they should make any conscience of what they do there, but they are only intent how to reimburse themselves (if their elections were at their own charge) or how to bargain their votes for a place or a pension. They list themselves straightways into some Court faction, and it is as well-known among them, to what Lord each of them retain, as when formerly they wore coats and badges. By this long haunting so together, they are grown too so familiar among themselves, that all reverence of their own Assembly is lost, that they live together not like Parliament men, but like so many good fellows met together in a publick house to make merry. And which is yet worse, by being so thoroughly acquainted, they understand their number and party, so that the use of so publick a counsel is frustrated, there is no place for deliberation, no perswading by reason, but they can see one another's votes through both throats and cravats before they hear them.

"Where the cards are so well known, they are only fit for a cheat, and no fair gamester but would throw them under the table."[1]

It is a melancholy picture.

Here, perhaps, may be best inserted the story about the proffered bribe. The story is entitled to small credit, but as helping to swell and maintain a tradition concerning an historical character about whom little is positively known, it can hardly escape mention in any biography of Marvell. A pamphlet printed in Ireland (1754) supplies an easy flowing version of the tale.

"The borough of Hull, in the reign of Charles II., chose Andrew Marvell, a young gentleman of little or no fortune, and maintained him in London for the service of the public. His understanding, integrity, and spirit, were dreadful to the then infamous administration. Persuaded that he would be theirs for properly asking, they sent his old school-fellow, the Lord Treasurer Danby, to renew acquaintance with him in his garret. At parting, the Lord Treasurer, out of *pure affection*, slipped into his hand an order upon the treasury for £1000, and then went to his chariot. Marvell, looking at the paper, calls after the Treasurer, 'My Lord, I request another moment.' They went up again to the garret, and Jack, the servant boy, was called. 'Jack, child, what had I for dinner yesterday?' 'Don't you remember, sir? you had the little shoulder of mutton that you ordered me to bring from a woman in the market.' 'Very right, child.' 'What have I for dinner to-day?' 'Don't you know, sir, that you bid me lay by the *blade-bone to broil*.' ''Tis so, very right, child, go away.' 'My Lord, do you hear that? Andrew Marvell's dinner is provided; there's your piece of paper. I want it not. I knew the sort of kindness you intended. I live here to serve my constituents: the ministry may seek men for their purpose; *I am not one*.'"[1]

One more letter remains to be quoted:—

To William Ramsden, Esq.

"*June 10, 1678.*

"DEAR WILL,—I have time to tell you thus much of publick matters. The patience of the Scots, under their oppressions, is not to be paralleled in any history. They still continue their extraordinary and numerous, but peaceable, field conventicles. One Mr. Welch is their arch-minister, and the last letter I saw tells, people were going forty miles to hear him. There came out, about Christmas last, here, a large book concerning the growth of popery and arbitrary government. There have been great rewards offered in private, and considerable in the Gazette, to any one who could inform of the author or printer, but not yet discovered. Three or four printed books since have described, as near as it was proper to go, the man being a Member of Parliament, Mr. Marvell, to have been the author; but if he had, surely he should not have escaped being questioned in Parliament or some other place. My good wishes attend you."

The last letter Andrew Marvell wrote to his constituents is dated July 6, 1678. The member for Hull died in August 1678. The Parliament in which he had sat continuously for eighteen years was at last dissolved on the 30th of December in the year of his death.

[181:1] Grosart, vol. iv. p. 248.

[183:1] Ranke's *History of England*, vol. iii. p. 471.

[185:1] Ranke, vol. iii. p. 520.

[187:1] Grosart, vol. iv. (*Growth of Popery*), p. 275.

[187:2] *Ibid.*, p. 279.

[189:1] See note to Dr. Airy's edition of Burnet's *History*, vol. ii. p. 73.

[199:1] Marvell's commendatory verses on "Mr. Milton's Paradise Lost" (so entitled in the volume of 1681) were first printed in the Second Edition (1674) of Milton's great poem. Marvell did not agree with Dryden in thinking that *Paradise Lost* would be improved by rhyme, and says so in these verses.

[202:1] Printed in Captain Thompson's edition, vol. i. p. 432.

[204:1] Grosart, vol. iv. p. 304.

[205:1] Grosart, vol. iv. p. 308.

[206:1] Grosart, vol. iv. p. 322.

[209:1] Grosart, vol. iv. p. 327.

[210:1] This story is first told in a balder form by Cooke in his edition of 1726. It may be read as Cooke tells it in the *Dictionary of National Biography*, xxxvi., p. 329. There was probably some foundation for it.

CHAPTER VII

FINAL SATIRES AND DEATH

MARVELL was no orator or debater, and though a member of Parliament for nearly eighteen years, but rarely opened his mouth in the House of Commons. His old enemy, Samuel Parker, whilst venting his posthumous spite upon the author of the *Rehearsal Transprosed*, would have us believe "that our Poet could not speak without a sound basting: whereupon having frequently undergone this discipline, he learnt at length to hold his tongue." There is no good reason for believing the Bishop of Oxford, but it is the fact that, however taught, Marvell had learnt to hold his tongue. His longest reported speech will be found in the *Parliamentary History*, vol. iv. p. 855.[1] When we remember how frequently in those days Marvell's pet subjects were under fierce discussion, we must recognise how fixed was his habit of self-repression.

On one occasion only are we enabled to catch a glimpse of Marvell "before the Speaker." It was in March 1677, and is thus reported in the *Parliamentary History*, though no mention of the incident is made in the Journals of the House:—

"*Debate on Mr. Andrew Marvell's striking Sir Philip Harcourt, March 29.*—Mr. Marvell, coming up the house to his place, stumbling at Sir Philip Harcourt's foot, in recovering himself, seemed to give Sir Philip a box on the ear. The Speaker acquainting the house 'That he saw a box on the ear given, and it was his duty to inform the house of it,' this debate ensued.

"Mr. *Marvell*. What passed was through great acquaintance and familiarity betwixt us. He neither gave him an affront, nor intended him any. But the Speaker cast a severe reflection upon him yesterday, when he was out of the house, and he hopes that, as the Speaker keeps us in order, he will keep himself in order for the future.

"Sir *John Ernly*. What the Speaker said yesterday was in Marvell's vindication. If these two gentlemen are friends already, he would not make them friends, and would let the matter go no further.

"Sir *Job. Charlton* is sorry a thing of this nature has happened, and no more sense of it. You in the Chair, and a stroke struck! Marvell deserves for his reflection on you, Mr. Speaker, to be called in question. You cannot do right to the house unless you question it; and moves to have Marvell sent to the Tower.

"The *Speaker*. I saw a blow on one side, and a stroke on the other.

"Sir *Philip Harcourt*. Marvell had some kind of a stumble, and mine was only a thrust; and the thing was accidental.

"Sir *H. Goodrick*. The persons have declared the thing to be accidental, but if done in jest, not fit to be done here. He believes it an accident, and hopes the house thinks so too.

"Mr. Sec. *Williamson*. This does appear, that the action for that time was in some heat. He cannot excuse Marvell who made a very severe reflection on the Speaker, and since it is so enquired, whether you have done your duty, he would have Marvell withdraw, that you may consider of it.

"Col. *Sandys*. Marvell has given you trouble, and instead of excusing himself, reflects upon the Speaker: a strange confidence, if not an impudence!

"Mr. *Marvell*. Has so great a respect to the privilege, order, and decency, of the house, that he is content to be a sacrifice for it. As to the casualty that happened, he saw a seat empty, and going to sit in it, his friend put him by, in a jocular manner, and what he did was of the same nature. So much familiarity has ever been between them, that there was no heat in the thing. He is sorry he gave an offence to the house. He seldom speaks to the house, and if he commit an error, in the manner of his speech, being not so well tuned, he hopes it is not an offence. Whether out or in the house, he has a respect to the Speaker. But he has been informed that the Speaker resumed something he had said, with reflection. He did not think fit to complain of Mr. Seymour to Mr. Speaker. He believes that is not reflective. He desires to comport himself with all respect to the house. This passage with Harcourt was a perfect casualty, and if you think fit, he will withdraw, and sacrifice himself to the censure of the house.

"Sir *Henry Capel*. The blow given Harcourt was with his hat; the Speaker cast his eye upon both of them, and both respected him. He would not aggravate the thing. Marvell submits, and he would have you leave the thing as it is.

"*Sir Robert Holmes* saw the whole action. Marvell flung about three or four times with his hat, and then gave Harcourt a box on the ear.

"Sir *Henry Capel* desires, now that his honour is concerned, that Holmes may explain, whether he saw not Marvell with his hat only give Harcourt the stroke 'at that time.' Possibly 'at another time' it might be.

"The *Speaker*. Both Holmes and Capel are in the right. But Marvell struck Harcourt so home, that his fist, as well as his hat, hit him.

"Sir *R. Howard* hopes the house will not have Harcourt say he received a blow, when he has not. He thinks what has been said by them both sufficient.

"Mr. *Garraway* hopes, that by the debate we shall not make the thing greater than it is. Would have them both reprimanded for it.

"Mr. Sec. *Williamson* submits the honour of the house to the house. Would have them made friends, and give that necessary assurance to the house, and he, for his part, remains satisfied.

"Sir *Tho. Meres*. By our long sitting together, we lose, by our familiarity and acquaintance, the decencies of the house. He has seen 500 in the house, and people very orderly; not so much as to read a letter, or set up a foot. One could scarce know anybody in the house, but him that spoke. He would have the Speaker declare that order ought to be kept; but as to that gentleman (Marvell) to rest satisfied."

The general impression left upon the mind is that of a friendly-familiar but choleric gentleman, full of likes and dislikes, readier with his tongue in the lobby than with "set" speeches in the Chamber. A solitary politician with a biting pen. Satirists must not complain if they have enemies.

Marvell's vein of satire was never worked out, and the political poems of his last decade are fuller than ever of a savage humour. How he kept his ears is a repeated wonder. He is said to have been on terms of intimate friendship with Prince Rupert, and it is a steady tradition that the king was one of his amused readers. It is hard to believe that even Charles the Second could have seen any humour, good or bad, in such a couplet:—

"The poor Priapus King, led by the nose,
Looks as a thing set up to scare the crows."

Nor can the following verses have been read with much pleasure, either at Whitehall or in a punt whilst fishing at Windsor. Their occasion was the setting up in the stocks-market in the City of London of a statue of the king by Sir Robert Viner, a city knight, to whom Charles was very heavily in debt. Sir Robert, having a frugal mind, had acquired a statue of John Sobieski trampling on the Turk, which, judiciously altered, was made to pass muster so as to represent the Pensioner of Louis the Fourteenth and the Vendor of Dunkirk trampling on Oliver Cromwell.

"As cities that to the fierce conqueror yieldDo at their own charges their citadels build;So Sir Robert advanced the King's statue in tokenOf bankers defeated, and Lombard Street broken.

Some thought it a knightly and generous deed,Obliging the city with a King and a steed;When with honour he might from his word have gone back;He that vows in a calm is absolved by a wrack.

But now it appears, from the first to the last,
To be a revenge and a malice forecast;
Upon the King's birthday to set up a thing
That shows him a monkey much more than a King.

When each one that passes finds fault with the horse,
Yet all do affirm that the King is much worse;
And some by the likeness Sir Robert suspect
That he did for the King his own statue erect.

Thus to see him disfigured—the herb-women chid,
Who up on their panniers more gracefully rid;
And so loose in his seat—that all persons agree,
E'en Sir William Peak[1] sits much firmer than he.

But Sir Robert affirms that we do him much wrong;
'Tis the 'graver at work, to reform him, so long;
But, alas! he will never arrive at his end,
For it is such a King as no chisel can mend.

But with all his errors restore us our King,
If ever you hope in December for spring;
For though all the world cannot show such another,
Yet we'd rather have him than his bigoted brother."

Of a more exalted vein of satire the following extract may serve as an example:—

BRITANNIA AND RALEIGH

"*Brit.* Ah! Raleigh, when thou didst thy breath resign
To trembling James, would I had quitted mine.
Cubs didst thou call them? Hadst thou seen this brood
Of earls, and dukes, and princes of the blood,
No more of Scottish race thou would'st complain,
Those would be blessings in this spurious reign.
Awake, arise from thy long blessed repose,
Once more with me partake of mortal woes!

Ral. What mighty power has forced me from my rest?
Oh! mighty queen, why so untimely dressed?

Brit. Favoured by night, concealed in this disguise,
Whilst the lewd court in drunken slumber lies,
I stole away, and never will return,
Till England knows who did her city burn;
Till cavaliers shall favourites be deemed,
And loyal sufferers by the court esteemed;
Till Leigh and Galloway shall bribes reject;
Thus Osborne's golden cheat I shall detect:
Till atheist Lauderdale shall leave this land,
And Commons' votes shall cut-nose guards disband:
Till Kate a happy mother shall become,
Till Charles loves parliaments, and James hates Rome.

Ral. What fatal crimes make you for ever fly
Your once loved court, and martyr's progeny?

Brit. A colony of French possess the Court,
Pimps, priests, buffoons, i' the privy-chamber sport.
Such slimy monsters ne'er approached the throne
Since Pharaoh's reign, nor so defiled a crown.
I' the sacred ear tyrannic arts they croak,
Pervert his mind, his good intentions choke;
Tell him of golden Indies, fairy lands,
Leviathan, and absolute commands.
Thus, fairy-like, the King they steal away,
And in his room a Lewis changeling lay.
How oft have I him to himself restored.
In's left the scale, in 's right hand placed the sword?
Taught him their use, what dangers would ensue
To those that tried to separate these two?
The bloody Scottish chronicle turned o'er,
Showed him how many kings, in purple gore,
Were hurled to hell, by learning tyrant lore?
The other day famed Spenser I did bring,
In lofty notes Tudor's blest reign to sing;
How Spain's proud powers her virgin arms controlled,
And golden days in peaceful order rolled;
How like ripe fruit she dropped from off her throne,
Full of grey hairs, good deeds, and great renown....

Ral. Once more, great queen, thy darling strive to save,
Snatch him again from scandal and the grave;
Present to 's thoughts his long-scorned parliament,

The basis of his throne and government.
In his deaf ears sound his dead father's name:
Perhaps that spell may 's erring soul reclaim:
Who knows what good effects from thence may spring?
'Tis godlike good to save a falling king.

Brit. Raleigh, no more, for long in vain I've tried
The Stuart from the tyrant to divide;
As easily learned virtuosos may
With the dog's blood his gentle kind convey
Into the wolf, and make his guardian turn
To the bleating flock, by him so lately torn:
If this imperial juice once taint his blood,
'Tis by no potent antidote withstood.
Tyrants, like lep'rous kings, for public weal
Should be immured, lest the contagion steal
Over the whole. The elect of the Jessean line
To this firm law their sceptre did resign;
And shall this base tyrannic brood invade
Eternal laws, by God for mankind made?

To the serene Venetian state I'll go,
From her sage mouth famed principles to know;
With her the prudence of the ancients read,
To teach my people in their steps to tread;
By their great pattern such a state I'll frame,
Shall eternize a glorious lasting name.
Till then, my Raleigh, teach our noble youth
To love sobriety, and holy truth;
Watch and preside over their tender age,
Lest court corruption should their souls engage;
Teach them how arts, and arms, in thy young days,
Employed our youth—not taverns, stews, and plays;
Tell them the generous scorn their race does owe
To flattery, pimping, and a gaudy show;
Teach them to scorn the Carwells, Portsmouths, Nells,
The Clevelands, Osbornes, Berties, Lauderdales:
Poppaea, Tigelline, and Arteria's name,
All yield to these in lewdness, lust, and fame.
Make them admire the Talbots, Sydneys, Veres,
Drake, Cavendish, Blake, men void of slavish fears,
True sons of glory, pillars of the state,
On whose famed deeds all tongues and writers wait.

When with fierce ardour their bright souls do burn,
Back to my dearest country I'll return."

The dialogue between the two horses, which bore upon their respective backs the stone effigies of Charles the First at Charing Cross and Charles the Second at Wool-Church, is, in its own rough way, masterly satire for the popular ear.

"If the Roman Church, good Christians, oblige ye
To believe man and beast have spoken in effigy,
Why should we not credit the public discourses,
In a dialogue between two inanimate horses?
The horses I mean of Wool-Church and Charing,
Who told many truths worth any man's hearing,
Since Viner and Osborn did buy and provide 'em
For the two mighty monarchs who now do bestride 'em.
The stately brass stallion, and the white marble steed,
The night came together, by all 'tis agreed;
When both kings were weary of sitting all day,
They stole off, incognito, each his own way;
And then the two jades, after mutual salutes,
Not only discoursed, but fell to disputes."

The dialogue is too long to be quoted. Charles the Second's steed boldly declares:—

"De Witt and Cromwell had each a brave soul,
I freely declare it, I am for old Noll;
Though his government did a tyrant resemble,
He made England great, and his enemies tremble."

Mr. Hollis, when he sent the picture of Cromwell by Cooper to Sidney Sussex College, is said to have written beneath it the lines just quoted.

The satire ends thus:—

"*Charing Cross*. But canst them devise when things will be mended?

Wool-Church. When the reign of the line of the Stuarts is ended.

Charing Cross. Then England, rejoice, thy redemption draws nigh;
Thy oppression together with kingship shall die.

Chorus. A Commonwealth, a Commonwealth we proclaim to the nation,For the gods have repented the King's restoration."

These probably are the lines which spread the popular, but mistaken, belief that Marvell was a Republican.

Andrew Marvell died in his lodgings in London on the 16th of August 1678. Colonel Grosvenor, writing to George Treby, M.P. (afterwards Chief of the Common Pleas), on the 17th of August, reports "Andrew Marvell died yesterday of apoplexy." Parliament was not sitting at the time. What was said of the elder Andrew may also be said of the younger: he was happy in the moment of his death. The one just escaped the Civil War, the other the Popish Plot.

Marvell was thought to have been poisoned. Such a suspicion in those bad times was not far-fetched. His satires, rough but moving, had been widely read, and his fears for the Constitution, his dread of

"The grim Monster, Arbitrary Power,
The ugliest Giant ever trod the earth,"

infested many breasts, and bred terror.

"Marvell, the Island's watchful sentinel,
Stood in the gap and bravely kept his post."

The post was one of obvious danger, and

"Whether Fate or Art untwin'd his thread
Remains in doubt."[1]

The doubt has now been dissipated by the research of an accomplished physician, Dr. Gee, who in 1874 communicated to the *Athenæum* (March 7, 1874) an extract from Richard Morton's Πυρετολογία (1692), containing a full account of Marvell's sickness and death. Art "untwin'd his thread," but it was the doctor's art. Dr. Gee's translation of Morton's medical Latin is as follows:—

"In this manner was that most famous man Andrew Marvell carried off from amongst the living before his time, to the great loss of the republic, and especially the republic of letters; through the ignorance of an old conceited doctor, who was in the habit on all occasions of raving excessively against Peruvian bark, as if it were a common plague. Howbeit, without any clear indication, in the interval after a third fit of regular tertian ague, and by way of preparation (so that all things might seem to be done most methodically), blood was copiously drawn from the patient, who was advanced in years." [Here follow more details of treatment, which I pass over.] "The way having been made ready after this fashion, at the beginning of the next fit, a great febrifuge was given, a draught, that is to say, of Venice treacle, etc. By the doctor's orders, the patient was covered up close with blankets, say rather, was buried under them; and composed himself to sleep and sweat, so that he might escape the cold shivers which are wont to accompany the onset of the ague-fit. He was seized with the deepest sleep and colliquative sweats, and in the short space of twenty-four hours from the time of the ague-fit, he died comatose. He died, who, had a single ounce of Peruvian bark been properly given, might easily have escaped, in twenty-four hours, from the jaws of the grave and the disease: and so burning with anger, I informed the doctor, when he told me this story without any sense of shame."

Marvell was buried on the 18th of August, "under the pews in the south side of St. Giles's Church in the Fields, under the window wherein is painted on glass a red lion." So writes the invaluable Aubrey, who tells us he had the account from the sexton who made the grave.

In 1678 St. Giles's Church was a brick structure built by Laud. The present imposing church was built on the site of the old one in 1730-34.

In 1774 Captain Thompson, so he tells us, "visited the grand mausoleum under the church of St. Giles, to search for the coffin in which Mr. Marvell was placed: in this vault were deposited upwards of a thousand bodies, but I could find no plate of an earlier date than 1722; I do therefore suppose the new church is built upon the former burial place."

The poet's grand-nephew, Mr. Robert Nettleton, in 1764 placed on the north side of the present church, upon a black marble slab, a long epitaph, still to be seen, recording the fact that "near to this place lyeth the body of Andrew Marvell, Esquire." At no great distance from this slab is the tombstone, recently brought in from the graveyard outside, of *Georgius Chapman, Poeta*, a fine Roman monument, prepared by the care and at the cost of the poet's friend, Inigo Jones. Still left exposed, in what is now a doleful garden (not at all Marvellian), is the tombstone of Richard Penderel of Boscobel, one of the five yeomen brothers who helped Charles to escape after Worcester. Lord Herbert of Cherbury, in 1648, and Shirley the dramatist, in 1666, had been carried to the same place of sepulture.

Aubrey describes Marvell "as of middling stature, pretty strong-set, roundish faced, cherry-cheeked, hazell eye, brown hair. He was, in his conversation, very modest, and of very few words. Though he loved wine, he would never drink hard in company, and was wont to say that he would not play the good fellow in any man's company in whose hands he would not trust his life. He kept bottles of wine at his lodgings, and many times he would drink liberally by himself and to refresh his spirit and exalt his muse. James Harrington (author of *Oceana*) was his intimate friend; J. Pell, D.D., was one of his acquaintances. He had not a general acquaintance."

Dr. Pell, one may remark, was a great friend of Hobbes.

In March 1679 joint administration was granted by the Prerogative Court of Canterbury, *Mariæ Marvell relictæ et Johni Greni Creditori*. This is the first time we hear of there being any wife in the case. A creditor of a deceased person could not obtain administration without citing the next of kin, but a widow was entitled, under a statute of Henry VIII., as of right, to administration, and it may be that Mr. Green thought the quickest way of being paid his debt was to invent a widow. The practice of the court required an affidavit from the widow deposing that she was the lawful relict of the deceased, but this assertion on oath seems in ordinary cases to have been sufficient, if the customary fees were forthcoming. Captain Thompson roundly asserts that the alleged Mary Marvell was a cheat, and no more than the lodging-house keeper where he had last lived—and Marvell was a migratory man.[1] Mary Marvell's name appears once again, in the forefront of the first edition of Marvell's *Poems* (1681), where she certifies all the contents to be her husband's works. This may have been a publisher's, as the affidavit may have been a creditor's, artifice. As against this, Mr. Grosart, who believed in Mary Marvell, reminds us that Mr. Robert Boulter, the publisher of the poems, was a most respectable man, and a friend both of Milton's and Marvell's, and not at all likely either to cheat the public with a falsely signed certificate, or to be cheated by a London lodging-house keeper. Whatever "Mary Marvell" may have been, "widow, wife, or maid," she is heard of no more.

Hull was not wholly unmindful of her late and (William Wilberforce notwithstanding) her most famous member. "On Thursday the 26th of September 1678, in consideration of the kindness the Town and Borough had for Andrew Marvell, Esq., one of the Burgesses of Parliament for the same Borough (lately deceased), and for his great merits from the Corporation. It is this day ordered by the Court that Fifty pounds be paid out of the Town's Chest towards the discharge of his funerals (*sic*), and to perpetuate his memory by a gravestone" (*Bench Books of Hull*).

The incumbent of Trinity Church is said to have objected to the erection of any monument. At all events there is none. Marvell had many enemies in the Church. Sharp, afterwards Archbishop of York, was a Yorkshire man, and had been domestic chaplain to Sir Heneage Finch, a lawyer-member, much lashed by Marvell's bitter pen. Sharp had also taken part in the quarrel with the Dissenters, and is reported to have been very much opposed to any Hull monument to Marvell. Captain Thompson says "the Epitaph which the

Town of Hull caused to be erected to Marvell's memory was torn down by the Zealots of the King's party." There is no record of this occurrence.

There are several portraits of Marvell in existence—one now being in the National Portrait Gallery. A modern statue in marble adorns the Town Hall of Hull.

[211:1] In reading the early volumes of the *Parliamentary History* the question has to be asked, What authority is there for the reports of speeches? In Charles the Second's time some of the speakers, both in the Lords and Commons, evidently communicated their orations to the press.

[215:1] Lord Mayor, 1667.

[220:1] See *Marvell's Ghost*, in *Poems on Affairs of State*.

[223:1] The cottage at Highgate, long called 'Marvell's Cottage,' has now disappeared. Several of Marvell's letters were written from Highgate.

CHAPTER VIII

WORK AS A MAN OF LETTERS

MARVELL'S work as a man of letters easily divides itself into the inevitable three parts. *First*, as a poet properly so called; *Second*, as a political satirist using rhyme; and *Third*, as a writer of prose.

Upon Marvell's work as a poet properly so called that curious, floating, ever-changing population to whom it is convenient to refer as "the reading public," had no opportunity of forming any real opinion until after the poet's death, namely, when the small folio of 1681 made its appearance. This volume, although not containing the *Horatian Ode upon Cromwell's Return from Ireland* or the lines upon Cromwell's death, did contain, saving these exceptions, all the best of Marvell's verse.

How this poetry was received, to whom and to how many it gave pleasure, we have not the means of knowing. The book, like all other good books, had to take its chance. Good poetry is never exactly unpopular—its difficulty is to get a hearing, to secure a *vogue*. I feel certain that from 1681 onwards many ingenuous souls read *Eyes and Tears*, *The Bermudas*, *The Nymph complaining for the Death of her Fawn*, *To his Coy Mistress*, *Young Love*, and *The Garden* with pure delight. In 1699 the poet Pomfret, of whose *Choice* Dr. Johnson said in 1780, "perhaps no composition in our language has been oftener perused," and who Southey in 1807 declared to be "the most popular of English poets"; in 1699, I say, this poet Pomfret says in a preface, sensibly enough, "to please everyone would be a New Thing, and to write so as to please no Body would be as New, for even Quarles and Wythers (*sic*) have their Admirers." So liable is the public taste to fluctuations and reversals, that to-day, though Quarles and Wither are not popular authors, they certainly number many more readers than Pomfret, Southey's "most popular of English poets," who has now, it is to be feared, finally disappeared even from the Anthologies. But if Quarles and Wither had their admirers even in 1699, the poet Marvell, we may be sure, had his also.

Marvell had many poetical contemporaries—five-and-twenty at least—poets of mark and interest, to most of whom, as well as to some of his immediate predecessors, he stood, as I must suppose, in some degree of poetical relationship. With Milton and Dryden no comparison will suggest itself, but with Donne and Cowley, with Waller and Denham, with Butler and the now wellnigh forgotten Cleveland, with Walker and Charles Cotton, with Rochester and Dorset, some resemblances, certain influences, may be found and traced. From the order of his mind and his prose style, I should judge Marvell to have been both a reader and a critic of his contemporaries in verse and prose—though of his criticisms little remains. Of Butler he twice speaks with great respect, and his sole reference to the dead Cleveland is kindly. Of Milton we know what he thought, whilst Aubrey tells us that he once heard Marvell say that the Earl of Rochester was the only man in England that had the true vein of satire.

Be these influences what they may or must have been, to us Marvell occupies, as a poet, a niche by himself. A finished master of his art he never was. He could not write verses like his friend Lovelace, or like Cowley's *Chronicle* or Waller's lines "On a Girdle." He had not the inexhaustible, astonishing (though tiresome) wit of Butler. He is often clumsy and sometimes almost babyish. One has frequently occasion to wonder how a man of business could allow himself to be tickled by such obvious straws as are too many of the conceits which give him pleasure. To attribute all the conceits of this period to the influence of Dr. Donne is but a poor excuse after all. The worst thing that can be said against poetry is that there is so much tedium in it. The glorious moments are all too few. It is his honest recognition of this woeful fact that makes Dr. Johnson, with all his faults lying thick about him, the most consolatory of our critics to the ordinary reading man. "Tediousness is the most fatal of all faults.... Unhappily this pernicious failure is that which an author is least able to discover. We are seldom tiresome to ourselves.... Perhaps no man ever thought a line superfluous when he wrote it" (*Lives of the Poets*. Under *Prior*—see also under *Butler*).

That Marvell is never tiresome I will not assert. But he too has his glorious moments, and they are all his own. In the whole compass of our poetry there is nothing quite like Marvell's love of gardens and woods, of meads and rivers and birds. It is a love not learnt from books, not borrowed from brother-poets. It is not indulged in to prove anything. It is all sheer enjoyment.

"Bind me, ye woodbines, in your twines,
Curb me about, ye gadding vines,
And oh, so close your circles lace,
That I may never leave this place!
But, lest your fetters prove too weak,
Ere I your silken bondage break,
Do you, O brambles, chain me too,
And, courteous briars, nail me through....
Here at the fountain's sliding foot,
Or at some fruit-tree's mossy root,
Casting the body's vest aside,
My soul into the boughs does glide;
There, like a bird, it sits and sings."

No poet is happier than Marvell in creating the impression that he made his verses out of doors.

"He saw the partridge drum in the woods;
He heard the woodcock's evening hymn;
He found the tawny thrush's broods,
And the shy hawk did wait for him.
What others did at distance hear
And guessed within the thicket's gloom
Was shown to this philosopher,
And at his bidding seemed to come."

(From Emerson's *Wood Notes*.)

Marvell's immediate fame as a true poet was, I dare say, obscured for a good while both by its original note (for originality is always forbidding at first sight) and by its author's fame as a satirist, and his reputation as a lover of "liberty's glorious feast." It was as one of the poets encountered in the *Poems on Affairs of State* (fifth edition, 1703) that Marvell was best known during the greater part of the eighteenth century. As Milton's friend Marvell had, as it were, a side-chapel in the great Miltonic temple. The patriotic member of Parliament, who refused in his poverty the Lord-Treasurer Danby's proffered bribe, became a character in history before the exquisite quality of his garden-poetry was recognised. There was a cult for Liberty in the middle of the eighteenth century, and Marvell's name was on the list of its professors. Wordsworth's sonnet has preserved this tradition for us.

"Great men have been among us; hands that penn'd
And tongues that utter'd wisdom, better none:
The later Sydney, Marvell, Harrington."

In 1726 Thomas Cooke printed an edition of Marvell's works which contains the poetry that was in the folio of 1681, and in 1772 Cooke's edition was reprinted by T. Davies. It was probably Davies's edition that Charles Lamb, writing to Godwin on Sunday, 14th December 1800, says he "was just going to possess": a notable addition to Lamb's library, and an event in the history of the progress of Marvell's poetical reputation. Captain Thompson's edition, containing the *Horatian Ode* and other pieces, followed in 1776. In the great Poetical Collection of the Booksellers (1779-1781) which they improperly[1] called "Johnson's *Poets*" (improperly, because the poets were, with four exceptions, the choice not of the biographer but of the booksellers, anxious to retain their imaginary copyright), Marvell has no place. Mr. George Ellis, in his *Specimens* of the early English poets first published in 1803, printed from Marvell *Daphne and Chloe* (in part) and *Young Love*. When Mr. Bowles, that once famous sonneteer, edited Pope in 1806, he, by way of belittling Pope, quoted two lines from Marvell, now well known, but unfamiliar in 1806:—

"And through the hazels thick espy
The hatching throstle's shining eye."

He remarked upon them, "the last circumstance is new, highly poetical, and could only have been described by one who was a real lover of nature and a witness of her beauties in her most solitary retirement." On this Mark Pattison makes the comment that the lines only prove that Marvell when a boy went bird-nesting (*Essays*, vol. ii. p. 374), a pursuit denied to Pope by his manifold infirmities. The poet Campbell, in his *Specimens* (1819), gave an excellent sketch of Marvell's life, and selected *The Bermudas*, *The Nymph and Fawn*, and *Young Love*. Then came, fresh from talk with Charles Lamb, Hazlitt, with his *Select Poets* (1825), which contains the *Horatian Ode*, *Bermudas*, *To his Coy Mistress*, *The Nymph and Fawn*, *A Drop of Dew*, *The Garden*, *The Gallery*, *Upon the Hill and Grove at Billborow*. In this choice we may see the hand of Charles Lamb, as Tennyson's may be noticed in the selection made in Palgrave's *Golden Treasury* (1863). Dean Trench in his *Household Book of English Poetry* (1869) gives *Eyes and Tears*, the *Horatian Ode*, and *A Drop of Dew*. In Mr. Ward's *English Poets* (1880) Marvell is represented by *The Garden*, *A Drop of Dew*, *The Bermudas*, *Young Love*, the *Horatian Ode*, and the *Lines on Paradise Lost*. Thanks to these later Anthologies and to the quotations from *The Garden* and *Upon Appleton House* in the *Essays of Elia*, Marvell's fame as a true poet has of recent years become widespread, and is now, whatever vicissitudes it may have endured, well established.

As a satirist in rhyme Marvell has shared the usual and not undeserved fate of almost all satirists of their age and fellow-men. The authors of lines written in heat to give expression to the anger of the hour may well be content if their effusions give the pain or teach the lesson they were intended to give or teach. If you lash the age, you do so presumably for the benefit of the age. It is very hard to transmit even a fierce and genuine indignation from one age to another. Marvell's satires were too hastily composed, too roughly constructed, too redolent of the occasion, to enter into the kingdom of poetry. To the careful and character-loving reader of history, particularly if he chance to have a feeling for the House of Commons, not merely as an institution, but as a place of resort, Marvell's satirical poems must always be intensely interesting. They strike me as honest in their main intention, and never very wide of the mark. Hallam says, in his lofty way, "We read with nothing but disgust the satirical poetry of Cleveland, Butler, Oldham, Marvell," and he adds, "Marvell's satires are gross and stupid."[1] Gross they certainly occasionally are, but stupid they never are. Marvell was far too well-informed a politician and too shrewd a man ever to be stupid.

As a satirist Marvell had, if he wanted them, many models of style, but he really needed none, for he just wrote down in rough-and-ready rhyme whatever his head or his spleen suggested to his fancy. Every now and again there is a noble outburst of feeling, and a couplet of great felicity. I confess to taking great pleasure in Marvell's satires.

As a prose writer Marvell has many merits and one great fault. He has fire and fancy and was the owner and master of a precise vocabulary well fitted to clothe and set forth a well-reasoned and lofty argument. He knew how to be both terse and diffuse, and can compress himself into a line or expand over a paragraph. He has touches of a grave irony as well as of a boisterous humour. He can tell an anecdote and elaborate a parable. Swift, we know, had not only Butler's *Hudibras* by heart, but was also (we may be sure) a close student of Marvell's prose. His great fault is a very common one. He is too long. He forgets how quickly a reader grows tired. He is so interested in the evolutions of his own mind that he forgets his audience. His interest at times seems as if it were going to prove endless. It is the first business of an author to arrest and then to retain the attention of the reader. To do this requires great artifice.

Among the masters of English prose it would be rash to rank Marvell, who was neither a Hooker nor a Taylor. None the less he was the owner of a prose style which some people think the best prose style of all—that of honest men who have something to say.

[229:1] "Indecently" is the doctor's own expression.

[231:1] See Hallam's *History of Literature*, vol. iv. pp. 433, 439.